S.O.B.E.R.*
*Son Of A Bitch Everything's Real

*A Story of Addiction Told
By A Mother And Her Son*

ANITA BAGLANEAS DEVLIN
AND MICHAEL DEVLIN JR.

ISBN: 0692331476
ISBN 13: 9780692331477

*SON OF A BITCH—EVERYTHING'S REAL

Anita

I can tell you the exact moment I felt the *SOBER* fingers snapping in my face. My eyes were forced wide open the moment I stopped denying my reality. I was sitting in the car with my husband, driving our son to rehab. The rain was pounding against the car, yet it was creating a sense of silence for which I was grateful. Staring out the window, turned away from my husband, tears dripped almost as if in slow motion down my cheeks. I didn't want to hear anything but the rain. I only wanted to be alone and to *feel*.

I couldn't hang up the phone, I couldn't put down the book, and I couldn't change the channel. This was happening, and it was real.

Mike

This is the moment when I realized truth, truth in the face of sudden fear of what is really going on in my life and what is to come. It isn't just one moment but many moments where I have sat afraid of the very sensation itself. In these moments I have made a commitment not to run from the realities in life but instead to persevere, even if I am not so sure I still want to uphold that commitment. In the past I had never let myself reach this moment. Instead I kept myself in my own delusional reality of what I wanted by drowning myself in drugs, in turn never having to reach this moment of *feeling*.

I cannot remember the specific moment I first felt this. What is important is what I do when I come to this sensation: run away again, or learn to struggle well and march on.

This is the moment when I realized, "Son of a bitch—everything's real."

CONTENTS

FOREWORD

Chico West, LPCS
—Owner of Gaston House Transitional Living

Having worked in the addiction treatment field since 1994 as a therapist, interventionist, and owner of a transitional living home, I have had the pleasure of serving thousands of families throughout all stages of addiction and recovery. My experience has consistently demonstrated that the disease of addiction is a family one, taking its toll not only on the individual addict but also on his or her loved ones and caregivers. Some of the most difficult conversations I am called to conduct are those in which—despite open acknowledgment of a son or daughter's illness—a family is unwilling or unable to see that they too have grown sick over the course of their child's active addiction.

Anita Devlin was no exception—a mother who loved her son, Mike, deeply, despite having borne the brunt of much of the consequences caused by his addiction to painkillers. Following the tumult of getting Mike into treatment, Anita was faced with yet another hurdle: a confrontation with the truth that she herself needed to get healthy as well and learn to let go. I am overjoyed to say that she rose to the occasion and is today a changed woman, equipped with the knowledge and willingness to help other families along the same path of recovery.

SOBER offers a personal vantage point into not only the heartbreaking challenge of a child's addiction but also the hope and joy realized by those families who surrender, seek direction, and find recovery. I would recommend that any family, whether currently seeking treatment or still suffering the pain of loving an addict, take the time to read Anita's inspiring story of hope in the face of the seemingly hopeless. Her experience, though her own, will provide insight and fellowship for any parent, caregiver, child, or sibling faced with the disease of addiction.

INTRODUCTION

Does being a mother give us the right to think we can negotiate with God for our children? When I found out my son was addicted to pain pills, I did just that. I went to church and pleaded, "God, I don't care what happens to me; please just take care of my son."

My father was a Greek Orthodox priest, and I grew up to be a typical Greek mother. I love my family more than anything else in life. I especially love carrying on the traditions of my religion, cooking my grandmother's recipes for the holidays, and filling my home with family and friends. I thought the aromas of cinnamon and oregano wafting through the air wrapping its warmth around us would keep us safe from the big bad world outside our home.

It would protect us, especially from things like addiction.

The faith I had grown up with started slipping through my fingers. I stopped going to church and doing charity work. I stopped doing everything that made me feel good. I focused only on my son's addiction and unknowingly neglected my beautiful daughter. I let go of everything that made me strong until I had nothing to hold on to but fear. I feared what would happen if I focused on anything but him.

Do all moms put their children before themselves at any cost, and do all moms live their lives thinking, "I'm not OK if you're not OK"?

I shared my children's joy and sadness from the moment they were born. I was like so many other mothers who thought their children couldn't live without them. Mothers are the confidants who get the first call when something good happens and are the first ones who get the call when something is wrong.

Being codependent on each other suggests we aren't allowed to be there for our children without it being called some ugly word. Where do we draw the line between being labeled over bearing and wanting everything to be OK for our kids?

I'll tell you exactly where that line is. It's when we stop taking care of ourselves to take care of them. Loving your child at the expense of everything else can be an addiction in itself.

I finally understood the saying that a mother is only as happy as her saddest child. I felt so lost and confused, yet I couldn't talk to anyone about it. I was that parent who was petrified of being judged and that fear could have caused me to almost lose my son.

I had a typical middle class family and I had a son addicted to drugs. I found myself wondering, "Has the middle class become the 'middle child' of addiction? The one that nobody talks about?"

Or is it because our children were buffered from words like *addiction* and *drug abuse* in their "social" cocktail-hour suburban homes?

This is a story of hope. It is the story of my family's journey through my son's addiction and recovery told by my son, myself and at times my daughter. Hopefully it will help other mothers find the strength to come out of their closets of denial and seek help. Instead of being afraid of what people will think, they will think of the cost of doing nothing. Keeping the secret of addiction is exhausting and dangerous.

My family is not foolish enough to believe that relapse is not a possibility. Our eyes are no longer closed. We have painfully learned that addiction is an octopus with tentacles than can wrap itself around us and choke the life out of everything we love.

Everything is real.

Dedicated to those who never left our side

It is especially dedicated to Aunt Sophia, Uncle Nick and Johanne

CHAPTER 1

NO ONE CAN HELP ME

Anita

It was time to pack up the memories. I had come to Cape Cod for the weekend to box up the family home. After almost twenty years, it was time to sell and time to let go. It was a financial necessity. My husband, Michael, and I had been living in New York City for the last two years and had been renting out our cape house during the summer months.(I will refer to my husband as Michael and to my son as Mike to avoid confusion). Our daughter, Alex, had moved to Los Angeles to pursue her career, and our son, Mike, was attending the University of Vermont. I had woken up feeling just like the gloomy, gray sky outside my windows. Our beautiful home, which was once filled with noise and laughter, now sat quiet and empty before me. I was on edge that morning, feeling that something wasn't quite right. Perhaps it was because I was anxious about the future. I've always had

1

a hard time letting go, and selling my family home was extremely painful for me. Trying to delay the emptying of closets and going through generations of belongings, I threw on my boots and rain jacket and headed out to grab a few things at the market.

I still remember where I was, the exact aisle in the grocery store and what sat on the shelves, when my phone rang. "Hey, Mom. I think there's something wrong with Mike," Alex said.

"What?" I stopped. There was something about the adult tone she was using that made me very nervous. Frozen in place, I clutched the half-full shopping cart. I was afraid to let go.

"I don't know what's wrong. I'm worried. I just told Dad. His roommate called and said he can't find him. That no one knows where he is." I couldn't speak. There was a moment of heavy silence. "We need to find him," she pleaded.

It was the call I had been afraid of for a long time that I kept secretly hidden in my mind. The dread I kept locked up tight in a vault.

After hanging up I put my head down and walked to the exit. Nothing mattered except getting home and knowing my son was OK—not the shopping cart full of food and not my friend Mary, who saw me in the parking lot. I could hear her calling my name. She was only a few feet from me, but her voice echoed as if it was miles away, unable to penetrate the panic banging around in my head.

As I drove home, my daughter's words filled the car. *I'm worried. We need to find him.*

I walked back into the house and noticed that my hands were shaking. As I grabbed my phone to call Mike, my friend Sandy's name popped up on my phone. As much as I wanted to hear my son's voice, I was relieved. I wasn't ready to know the truth.

"Hey. I forgot my laptop at your house and have to come back." She had been staying with me and had left that morning for Boston.

"Oh, thank God. I need you. Please hurry," I said. As soon as we hung up, I called Mike. When I got his voicemail, I got angry. "Where the hell are you?" I screamed into the phone, tears streaming down my face. I sent him text messages demanding he call me. Once Sandy arrived, she put her hand on my arm and calmly said, "That's not going to work. Tell him you are worried about him and just want to make sure he's OK." She picked up my phone and handed it to me.

"Tell him you love him."

I told her there was no way I was doing that. He was being selfish by making everyone worry about him. He was being selfish by causing his sister so much grief. Sandy insisted though, and I sent what I later found out was the most important text I've ever sent in my entire life.

"Son, please let me know you are OK. I love you, and I need to know that you're OK."

Mike

I can remember sitting alone at the Motel 6 in Burlington. That Vermont motel was going to be the end of the road, or so I thought. I arrived there at night and had taken a few pills and done some coke. While I was in bed watching TV, wondering if I would sleep at all, I finally had what I wanted: to be alone.

I woke up to a snowy day. Not a nice, white, fluffy snow but a brown, wet sleet that made everything look dirty. The motel was quiet and gloomy. It felt like a secret hideout for refugees trying to stay under the radar. I could hear critters in the walls and ceiling that had come in to seek warmth and shelter from the cold.

Later that morning I listened to the voice mails and read the texts from my mother saying, "Where the hell are you?" and "Everyone is looking for you! You're going to rehab!" I loved my mother so very much, but the truth is that selfishness had taken over every aspect of my life. The only thought that crossed my mind was, "Why are they all looking for me? Is this about the kid I put in the hospital, or one of the people I had stolen from?"

Was I dreaming? Would I wake up? The truth was that I was wide awake, hoping it would all end. I did what I had always done before to ease the pain. After a simple phone call came a knock at the door, like clockwork. I spent my last chunk of change, which I had taken from a "friend's" dresser drawer. "He shouldn't have left it out," I told myself. "He basically begged me to take it from him."

A couple of hours and enough OxyContin to kill a small horse later, I found myself lying in the bathtub waiting for the heart palpitations to kill me. The walls were yellow and peeling, and the ceiling had mustard-colored splotches of mold everywhere. My mind was drifting and a memory of a warm spring day in my junior year of high school flooded my thoughts. I was the boy who scored the winning goal.

The fans were in greater numbers than usual because it was the second rivalry game between Barnstable and Falmouth. This time we were on Falmouth's turf. In our first game we absolutely destroyed them and it was a special day since our school had not beaten them in twelve years. They were wounded, ready to do whatever it took to survive. They wanted revenge.

Falmouth fought their hearts out, but so did we. There was no finesse or beauty in this game just raw and scrappy lacrosse. When I was on the field, especially in a game like that, adrenaline took hold of my whole body. My focus was on nothing but my task at hand. I was not nervous, anxious or scared. The final quarter ended in a tie and we moved to sudden death overtime. I took the opening faceoff.

The adrenaline encompassed my body completely. I was swift on the face off and knew that it was flawless. As I carried the ball down to setup into our offense, it was as if time slowed down. I thought about everything I was seeing, as if I were looking at a picture. As I thought about passing the ball around to create a play,

I saw Timmy and Josh working together on the crease with their sticks up ready to catch a pass from me to score. The defense had their sticks up hoping to knock down any pass through their area. The goalie was standing in a way that said, "There's no way any ball is getting in this net." And that's when I saw it.

Directly in front of me was the player I took the faceoff against. He was wide eyed and holding his stick out in front of him like a man holding a wooden chair out to keep a lion from coming closer. He was on his heels, and without confidence. At that moment I said to myself, "I'm going to score." I ran toward him, dodged to my left, and just as he thought he caught up to me, I rolled away from him. As I switched to my right hand I lowered the head of my stick down to the ground ready to pull the trigger.

As soon as I completed my roll, I pushed the ball toward the net while pulling my stick toward the sky. The ball sailed by Timmy and Josh, past the goalie's head, hit the bottom of the crossbar and found its way into the net. Sticks flew into the air and I was bombarded with praise and excitement. At that moment, I felt like the greatest person alive.

That game ended and so did the praise. No one was giving "poor little me" attention anymore and could only talk about what we were going to do that night. "But what about me? What about that game I just won twenty minutes ago?" These were the thoughts that went through my mind. I went from feeling like a king to making myself out to be a victim. I was on the bus ride back to school with my entire team, and I felt like the only one there. "No one understands me. I just won that game and they don't care. I don't need them anyway."

The sound of a rodent scurrying across the ceiling snapped me back to reality. I was no longer a high school lacrosse player; I was strung out, laying in a bathtub in a Motel 6.

My phone was off because that's how I made everything else disappear. For some reason I felt an urge to turn it on. "Dude, are you OK? I'm worried about you." "Hey man, don't worry about everything; just give me a shout." Pity? From these people whose trust I had abused and stolen from? I didn't want pity and concern. I wanted fear and respect. But why? For what? Did I really think I was that tough, even with nothing to my name while rotting in this cheap motel? That's when I saw it.

"Son, please just let me know you are OK…"

My mother? After all I'd put her through? She's still there? She's worried? Then I saw another message.

"Where are you? I love you, and I'm worried about you."

It was from Bob. After all I'd put one of my best friends through, he still cared enough to set aside the harm I'd done?

It was as if someone somewhere punched me square in the face and poured ice cold water down my back. Sheer surrender shrouded me, and those "to hell with-its" that always led to the next fix suddenly became a good thing. I was scared out of my mind and finally admitted to myself that I wasn't so tough. I needed my mother. I needed those who cared for me. I needed the people I had forcefully pushed away for so long. I sent my mother a text saying, "Mom, no one can help me."

I wanted to be a part of a family again and learn to live rather than be constantly waiting. It was then, as I polished off the rest of my pills, that I realized I wanted there to be a tomorrow. It was the first step. But it was sure as hell not going to be the last. That's when I made the call.

Anita

The sound of his voice erased any lingering anger. I felt guilty. I was his mother, and he needed me. "I'm scared, Mom. I'm scared and I need help," he said.

I closed my eyes and brought my hand to my mouth, trying to stifle the tears, trying to sound strong. "OK, honey. We're going to get you home. And we're going to get you help."

Mike told me he was in some cheap motel a few miles away from his school. As soon as we got off the phone, I called my husband. "Michael, you need to come home. Now."

"I spoke to Alex, and I'm already on my way," he said. "Mike is in trouble. He wants help. He needs help. He wants to come home." Michael was at work in New York, and I had the car on Cape Cod. That meant it would be another day and another night that my son would be alone. The idea of him scared and alone in that shithole hotel room was too much to bear.

I called Bob, one of Mike's best friends. I trusted him and asked if he could go and get Mike. Or at least spend the night there. Bob agreed.

I stood in my living room and stared out the window. I searched the blanket of snow covering the front yard for answers. I imagined what sort of state my son was in. Where he was. How he looked. The helplessness crept into my fingers and toes. It was all I could do to keep from shutting down while waiting for that call from Bob. I needed to know that Mike was safe. I needed to know that he was alive. I was losing it.

Dark and crazy thoughts started creeping into my mind. My faith had been challenged over the past few years and now my thoughts were spinning out of control, heading in a bad direction.

Why was this happening? Addiction wasn't supposed to happen to families like mine.

I've always believed that if I had faith in God then I would be protected from evil.

Because bad things were happening to my family, I felt weak and that my faith was being challenged.

The Greek in me took over. Did this weakness make me vulnerable? I started to wonder if someone had given my family the *mati*.

Giving someone the mati refers to casting the evil eye (*mati* being the Greek word for *eye*). The evil eye is a curse believed to be cast by a malevolent glare, usually given to a person when they are unaware. Many cultures believe that receiving the evil eye will cause misfortune or injury. Talismans created to protect against the evil eye are also frequently called "evil eyes."

I knew this belief went against the beliefs my religion had taught me. I was desperately searching for answers to something that made no sense to me. Little did I know that I would find out later that my thoughts were not so crazy.

I fell back into my normal routine to pass the time. I cleaned. I organized. Then I called Mike's roommate and thanked him for calling Alex. "You saved his life," I said over and over. "You saved my son's life."

While I tried to keep it together, Sandy called a few treatment centers around the country to get Mike a room. They were all booked. It would be weeks before anyone could take him. I never stopped to think about the fact that treatment centers were booked. I never stopped to think about how many other families were dealing with substance abuse. I was only focused on our situation. The insurance company was useless. They casually recommended a few local places as if we were tourists looking for a restaurant, and none of them specialized in dealing with young adults.

"He needs a place where he won't be lumped in with people twice his age," Sandy insisted. "A place for young adults."

After making a few calls, Sandy announced that the Caron Treatment Center in Pennsylvania would take him right away. When I realized that it was located only a few miles away from my aunt and uncle's home (my godparents), I felt a little more at ease. I wanted to feel something familiar in a very unfamiliar situation. For just a moment, I was relieved. Then she added, "It's going to cost thirty-five thousand dollars and they need it up front." I felt as if someone had punched me in the stomach.

I thought of my own mother. I had missed her so much since she passed away. She had managed every little aspect of our lives with such ease. She had always fixed everything. I wanted more than anything for her to plop herself down on my couch and tell me how to fix this. I wanted her to tell me how I could regain the control of my family that she never seemed to lose with hers. I needed my mother, and Mike needed me.

The fact that my father was a Greek Orthodox priest would have created an even bigger problem. I would have been petrified to share what was happening with him. Most Greeks don't talk about things like homosexuality or cancer, let alone addiction. I would have been forced to keep it all quiet because of my father's position. That would have been deadly. Keeping secrets is exhausting and helps no one. We talk about how close our big Greek families are and how we are always there for each other, but when your father is a priest, you have to be very careful of who you share things with.

I miss my father since he passed away, but I was grateful that I wouldn't have to worry about my family being judged by his parishioners. He was highly respected as a priest, but what a lot people seemed to overlook was that he was a father, a husband, and a grandfather as well. Although he listened every single day to his congregation's problems, secrets, and confessions, I think this would have crushed him. And, as I said before, Greeks don't talk about addiction. At least not the ones I know.

When my husband, Michael, finally got to the cape, he was exhausted. He looked as if it had been weeks since he'd slept, for fear of what would have changed once he woke up. I explained that we needed money to get Mike into the rehab center. He listened quietly, knowing it was too much. We just didn't have it. We were in the midst of a major financial crisis for the first time in our lives. When the stock market tanked, he had lost his job. He had only recently started working again at a new firm in New York City. I had a successful career selling real estate on Cape Cod for years, but my industry wasn't spared from the country's financial crisis either. Our lives were changing rapidly in every way imaginable.

I was so worried about my husband and how he was feeling or what he was thinking about. We were a team, but unlike me, he didn't like to talk about feelings and share his issues with anyone else. Michael has always been very private.

He was very close to his brothers, and I would constantly tell him to talk with them about the situation. I wanted him to talk and get his feelings out with someone he trusted, to feel some support. He was the youngest of eight, and I knew his brothers would be there for him to lean on, but he just wouldn't do it. I imagined he was feeling he'd be judged or that his son would be. I knew that would never be the case, but I couldn't push him. I had wasted so much time worrying about the same thing with my own family.

I did the only thing I could think of. I called Aunt Sophia and Uncle Nick.

When they arrived at our house, I didn't know what to expect. Maybe I hoped that my mother's little brother would instill a modicum of the calm I had felt with her. Maybe he would know, like she always did, what to do. As I sat there telling them what was going on, with Michael seemingly miles away on the other end of the couch, I realized I needed to be around family. My aunt Sophia was the closest person I had in my life besides my mother. She is my rock, the strongest woman I know. I have always shared things with her, and she would always guide me without passing judgment. She was my mother's best friend—I knew she missed her as much as I did.

I remember being with my mother, Aunt Sophia, and all the cousins at the beach in Cape Cod. Our days were filled with swimming lessons and ice blue popsicles, each of us wrapped up in matching beach towels. While the kids spent the entire day in the water, my mother and aunt would sit side by side in their beach chairs, keeping one eye on their children and one on each other. They were always talking and laughing, and now that I'm in my fifties, I get it. It's the sisterhood.

Aunt Sophia had married my mother's little brother, and these two amazing women were inseparable.

When I had finished talking, Aunt Sophia got up off the couch, got in her car, and drove away. I thought she was upset. I thought she was disappointed in me and needed to leave before saying something she would regret. She returned with a cashier's check in hand. Michael and I refused, insisting that we couldn't take their money. I told my uncle that we appreciated the gesture, but we couldn't possibly accept. It was too much.

He shook his head. "Remember years ago, when the restaurant was in trouble? You remember who was there to help us out? It was the two of you." Michael and I looked at each other. Neither of us had remembered. It felt like a lifetime ago. "Well that's what family does. And now it's our turn."

As lost and confused as I felt, their kindness anchored me to hope. I needed them. My son needed them. And they had been right there, ready to stand beside us and willing to do whatever it took to help.

As Michael pulled away for the trip to pick up Mike, I watched the brake lights from our silver Jeep disappear down the quiet residential street. The same road that just yesterday had felt immune to words like "addiction." My maternal instincts kicked in, and I began packing what I assumed we would need for the trip to Pennsylvania.

I wasn't sure what bringing-your-kid-to-rehab clothes were, but I was sure we didn't own them.

Regardless, I tried my best to keep busy, preparing my family for what lay ahead, no matter how badly I wished it would disappear. I started going through my old jewelry boxes trying to find the small evil eye pendants that I'd held on to for all those years, the same ones I had pinned to my babies' diapers to ward off evil. Perhaps now would be a good time to wear it. Perhaps it was too late.

Soon though, I ran out of things to keep me busy. Michael wouldn't be back for hours. I stood by the door, sobbing and waiting, wedged between the fear of what would come walking through the door when the Jeep's light's would once again appear in the driveway and the selfish desire to pass this whole damn thing off to someone else. Anyone else.

While Michael was driving to pick up Mike, we talked on the phone. He told me how frightened he was. He felt so helpless. Being the positive one, he was encouraged that Mike had decided to get help. At the same time, he was nervous about our son trying to make a run for it on the way home. He said his mind was racing in all different directions. I knew just how he felt.

When we hung up, I was overcome with exhaustion. I slumped down onto the floor. Sensing something was wrong, our bloodhound, Skilo, nuzzled next to me and rubbed her warm, wet snout against my hand while I wept. She stayed right there next to me, soaked from my tears, for what felt like weeks.

Then the door opened.

Skilo and I raised our heads at the familiar squeak of a Cape Cod screen door. Blood filled my body, and I jumped to my feet faster than I had in years, faster than I thought I still could at my age.

I didn't even want to look at Mike. I just wanted to hold him. That connection we had always shared broke through the hours of angst and trepidation. I squeezed him as hard as I could.

When we finally pulled away, I looked at his face and broke down all over again. This wasn't my son. His beautiful eyes had dulled into hollow caverns. I knew in that moment that as much as I wanted to be the solution, it would take more than just a mother's love to bring my son back.

Wrapping him up in the same quilt that had covered his bed since he was a child, rubbing his back, and making his favorite meal wasn't going to save his life.

I saw the toll all this had taken on my husband. He wasn't just tired. He looked scared, a helpless, broken shell of his former self. Though he barely spoke, he looked like I felt. This wasn't supposed to be our reality. It didn't make sense. This didn't happen to people like us.

But there we were, Mike's face hammering home how real it all was.

Mike

As I was nodding out in the motel bed, I heard a few bangs on my door. I opened it. "You look like death," Bob said as he wrapped his arms around me. I was feeling so frail that his hug was more painful than comforting. Maybe in some way Bob had wanted to hurt me for all that I had put everyone through.

The next morning, before we were to head out of Vermont to meet my father, I asked him if we could grab breakfast. I didn't even want food at that point. Nausea and chills were already kicking in from lack of dope in my body. My plan was to buy enough time to get loaded one more time before leaving. I knew Bob wouldn't let me, so I sent a text to the one person who I had not yet robbed. I told him to meet me on the backside of the breakfast place right over the Winooski River with the two sneakers hanging outside. I'd slip into the bathroom and out the window and grab what I needed. That was the plan. Of course, I had no money at the time, so I would have to tell the connect that I would "pay him back." He never made it on time anyway.

The car ride was a blur to me. I remember having some laughs with Bob and getting serious at times.

Ultimately, I ended up passing out for the majority of the ride. I woke up to my father at a train station, where I would continue my journey with him to Cape Cod. I don't recall how we ended up at certain places or when we'd left them. It all happened so quickly; perhaps I wasn't even conscious for most of it.

I remember my mother's face. It was pale and drained, as if she had seen a ghost. I think she hugged and kissed me, or I would assume that she did. I wanted help. I honestly did. I wanted to get clean with all my heart. This mental obsession and physical craving was just too great for me to overcome on my own. I needed my family.

I can't remember if it was that day or the next, but I did end up getting something to ease the pain. I started walking away from the house. My mother was suspicious and said something to me. I don't remember her exact words, but again I lied to her. I had to. I wish I hadn't, but I just did not have the willpower to refrain from getting loaded. I don't remember where I got the money, or if the person just helped me out for free. But I got just enough of it to ease the pain for the remaining time with my family.

Then, I was in New York City at our apartment. When did we leave Cape Cod? How long were we there? Were we even there? I knew the answer was yes because I still had what I needed to get me through these next couple of days. I was another day closer to Pennsylvania.

Motel 6 in Vermont. A train station in Connecticut. Cape Cod. New York City. Next stop, Pennsylvania, where I would clean up my life. Or maybe where I would be starting it. I didn't know what to expect next, and I didn't care. I just remember an overwhelming feeling of joy for some reason. Whether I was actually ready or I was just feeling content from the meds, it didn't matter. I was going in the same direction, regardless of the reason.

In the moments before we arrived at my great-aunt and great-uncle's house in Pennsylvania, I remember obsessing about what kind of meds they had stashed around their house. I remember feeling so selfish with these thoughts, but I could not stop them. However, the moment we pulled up and I saw Aunt Seva's wide, kind eyes, those thoughts were wiped from my mind. I felt as if I didn't need anything. My aunt Seva and uncle Al are such kind souls that their presence was greater than any relief I could get from a drug. I was so grateful to just be able to have lunch with them at a quaint little Greek diner before I was admitted.

That part of my trip I do remember.

Anita

I couldn't sleep the last night we spent on the cape. We would be leaving for New York City in the morning before going to Pennsylvania. Part of me still doubted Mike's desire to be helped, and I was afraid that he would run off during the night. So I stayed awake, keeping guard.

In the morning, when we drove back to the apartment in New York, no one spoke. Mike slept in the backseat, just as he had all those years ago as a kid.

The night before leaving for Pennsylvania, Mike wrote a letter to the head of admissions at UVM and left it on the kitchen table. I could feel his fear and desperation. He wasn't being forced into getting help. He wanted it. I knew I could sleep that night, because I knew he would be there when I woke up.

Dear ---,

I would like to thank you with all my heart for being so understanding through all of this. It has been a hairy ride for everyone, including myself, my friends, and most of all, my family. The battle has been a long one, and it will continue for a long time. I can genuinely say, however, that the number-one thing that I have to be most grateful for is the support of my family. Without their understanding and acceptance, I would not have the opportunity to once and for all break through this shell and rise above this nonsense. I owe it to not only myself, but my mother, father, and sister, who have stuck by my side through the worst and still continue to support me for who I am.

Every step, every choice, every fall has had to happen for me to end up where I am, and for once I feel confident and without worry.

So again, I thank you for your support and understanding, and I promise I will never give this fight up. I say this to you because even you, this time and last, have been a link in the chain to my future success. In the next steps, I would like my mother, Anita Devlin, and father, Michael Devlin, to be allowed full access to all of my school records, including my academic transcripts. Along with this, I will also be requesting a medical withdrawal from the university.

I must focus on myself as a human being, physically, socially, and mentally, before I can put myself onto the next track and decide where I will end up. One step at a time. I wish the best of luck to you, both in life and at the groovy UVM. I will truly miss all of you. Thanks again for everything, and have a great spring semester!

Sincerely,
Mike Devlin

CHAPTER 2

A WHOLE LOT OF SELF

Anita

As we made our way out of the city and onto the end-less highways toward Pennsylvania, I began to see deer after deer on the side of the road. So many times in the past, I had stopped and taken a wounded or dead animal off the highway, feeling no creature deserved to be left there like that. But there was no stopping now, and that filled me with rage. Perhaps I was angry no one else had stopped to collect the bodies. Or maybe feeling this emotion toward something that wasn't me, or my son, was my psyche's way of releasing the pressure building inside me before I exploded.

I gripped the hand rest and gritted my teeth, deter-mined to remain focused.

Through the entire three-hour car ride, I kept hop-ing the GPS would stop giving directions and yell at us to turn the hell around and go back to our regular lives. It never happened.

My godparents lived a few miles from the rehab center, and I had called them before leaving New York City to see about staying over. For some reason checking into a hotel felt wrong.

Though I'd been nervous about making the call and telling them about what had happened with Mike, as we inched closer to the uncertainty awaiting us, it was my godmother's words that comforted me. "Drive slow," she said. "Everything will be OK. We will get through this." The fact that she used the word *we* reminded me of how grateful I am for my family. I prayed her words would hold true. There were no options other than getting through this nightmare.

The morning after we arrived at my godparents' house, we took the ride to where Mike would be spending the next month of his life. Not being in control had me climbing the walls of the car. I was trying to remember when I first noticed a change in my son. I'm not sure why this was the time I chose to start this chaotic search through my mind. I can only assume that I was wondering if it was entirely my fault, wondering if I could have prevented any of this from happening—wondering if I had been a terrible mother.

From the time Mike was in middle school, we would get into heated arguments, with neither of us ever wanting to give in. I always assumed that he had my Greek blood pumping through his veins, and I actually admired his spirit. One day I sat down and wrote him a letter, placed it on his pillow, and waited to see if he would write me back.

I wrote him a letter because years earlier, a therapist told me that when you can't fix things face-to-face, you should sit down and write. I had been seeing a therapist back then about my own relationship with my father. I had things I needed to say to him during that time but couldn't. I thought the idea was foolish, and I also had no clue as to what I would say. Then one day I followed the therapist's advice and started typing a letter to my father. Seventeen pages later, and without stopping once, my shirt and lap were soaked through with tears. I printed it out and called my therapist, asking what I was supposed to do next. I couldn't give it to my father. He had dementia.

The therapist asked me if I had a special place that I would visit when I needed serenity. I actually did have a special place and can remember wondering if everyone had such a spot. She told me to go there and to bury the letter I held in my hand. I grabbed a shovel. I had buried every goose, chick, turtle, bird, and raccoon within a five-mile radius at the Buddha down by the stream. It was my own private pet cemetery. Each animal was carefully wrapped with a blanket and crosses were placed in each of their graves. It was my special place.

I started to dig a hole while uncontrollably sobbing. Emotions were pouring out from deep inside, where I'd hidden them years before. It was the same flood I'd felt when my mother died. The noises that were coming from deep inside of me were the same sounds I had made when she had passed away. They were the animalistic moans of grief and pain leaving my body. Once I finished covering the hole, I felt emotionally and physically exhausted. As the days passed, the emotion turned to relief.

That was a long time ago, but I can remember it like it happened this morning. This particular morning happened to be worse. We were driving to rehab, where I would be handing over my son.

As we turned in off the main road and headed up a beautiful, steep hill to what looked like a college campus, I thought about the day we'd dropped Mike off at the University of Vermont a few years earlier.

My friend Terri had come along to help, and it was a beautiful, early September day. I could feel the change in the air, the slight hint of summer turning to fall. It felt crisp and clean. A new chapter in life.

My youngest going off to college meant the end of an era as a mother. I wouldn't have to do all the things I had always complained about: cooking for my kids' friends, doing endless amounts of laundry, and always coming second in their lives. But I've had a problem my entire life of not living in the moment but instead fearing the future and things not happening as the way I had planned. I was the ultimate control freak, and instead of enjoying the day, I worried that I would be blamed if Mike didn't like this school.

He had wanted to go to Springfield, and I talked him into UVM.

I was afraid of so many different things that I felt nauseated the entire day. Change is supposed to be a good thing, but I was petrified, wondering what the hell I was going to do for the second half of my life. It was all I could think about after giving my son a hug and saying good-bye. I felt empty.

Even though the sun was shining and everything was neat and tidy, just like it had been at UVM that morning, I had to keep reminding myself that this was not college. It was rehab. Son Of a Bitch—Everything's Real kept slapping me in the face. This was happening. It was real.

I was handing my son over to strangers to help him. Behind those walls I had no control of keeping things in order and I felt like a failure because I hadn't been able to fix my son. I didn't want someone else to be the savior in my child's life. I'm a mother. and felt that if I can't help him, then no one can. I had no faith in anyone but myself. Thoughts were rushing through my mind now:

Who were these people?

How are they going to help him?

They don't even know him.

I felt as though I was losing my son, my faith, and my mind all at the same time. I was going deeper and deeper underwater trying to gasp for air, trying to reach for something to grab on to while trying not to drown.

At one time that would have been my faith, but at this point the only one I could have faith in was my son, and that frightened me. The realization that my son would have to commit to overcome this evil was devastating to me. My faith was challenged every way I turned. Where was my God? Who is my son? I had no answers. I only had questions surrounded by fear and uncertainty.

I looked in the rearview mirror at my son. He looked very serene and even had a bit of a smile on his face. Was his smile sincere, or was this just another manipulative move on his part? I was so done with letting him manipulate us and was also done with being the one that allowed it. I knew many times that he had been lying to us. I just didn't know how serious the situation was. I didn't know he was addicted to pills. I didn't know a damn thing.

We pulled into the admissions parking lot, and the three of us got out of the car. We walked to the building in silence. Watching my son interact with the girl at the front desk made me angry. Hearing him talk to the admissions counselor made me angry. Everything about being here made me want to scream and to grab and shake my son. I wished I could control my emotions and be the stoic person my husband was. He was calm and very attentive to everything that was going on around us. I knew this was the opportune time for me to make a quick escape. I excused myself and went to the ladies' room to compose myself. It was so ironic that Mike would be committing to stay here for a month, and I couldn't handle being there for an hour. I just stood against the wall in the ladies' room, sobbing. Staring down at the shiny tile floor, I decided to wash my face and clean up the mascara that was probably running down my face. Once I looked up, I realized I hadn't even put any makeup on that day. I took a long look in the mirror. It wasn't just Mike who had changed.

I didn't look like myself anymore either. There were new lines everywhere, wrinkles of worry, fear, anger, and denial that I never thought I'd see on my face. I felt dizzy. I was hopeful I wouldn't have to worry for a few weeks, knowing my son was safe in this place and getting the help he needed. But my anger wasn't so easily conquered. It lashed out in all directions before settling where I felt it really belonged.

"Is my denial the reason things have gotten so out of hand? Is it my fault that my son is here?" I could feel a new crease forming.

Its name was guilt.

Just as it was with my father all those years ago, the writing of letters back and forth between my son and me always ended our arguments. But I had no idea that this exchange of words on paper from our past would prove an educational exercise to prepare me for the writing of what's known in rehab as a "cost letter." The emotions surging through my veins in this bathroom would end up being a large part of my first letter to Mike.

I prepared myself for the daunting task of sitting down and writing my son a letter telling him exactly what he had cost us as a family. Not monetarily, but emotionally, mentally and every other which way. I didn't want to put those words on paper. It seemed cruel, especially as a mother.

I will never forget leaving my son behind on that day. It was eerily similar to when my brother John and I had taken my father, who had Alzheimer's, to an assisted living facility in Framingham, Massachusetts. The only difference was, I vividly remember my father having a confused look of terror in his eyes when he realized he wasn't coming with us. My son did not.

It was easier to deal with my own fears knowing I didn't have to worry about my son being terrified. We had no choice in the matter back then, but the decision was on my brother and me. Not my father. Alzheimer's was an ugly and dangerous disease. We had to make sure our father was in a safe place and being watched at all times. Just like my son. Unlike with my father, there was no guarantee Mike would stay in this place. He could leave anytime he wanted to.

Mike would be with strangers all day every day. My father was also, but my brother John was there with him all the time as well. There was a sense of calm knowing that my brother was on top of everything and knowing that he took better care of my father than everyone else put together. But I had no brother at the rehab to make sure my son was OK. I had to learn to trust people I didn't know. This was another avenue my mind would wander off to and worry about. My mind was a road map of worry.

Selfishly, I prayed for a break. I wanted these people to fix him and give him back to us like a car I had brought in to be serviced.

I wanted it to be easy. I had been smoking all the time and taking Ativan to try and sleep through the night. I rationalized my behavior by thinking it was my son's fault. He was the reason I was doing all these bad things. I felt so sorry for myself. I had lost my mother to breast cancer and my father shortly thereafter. My mother had ignored her symptoms, and I had ignored my son's. I would not find out until family therapy how close I had come to losing one of my children to the disease of addiction. I was tired and broken and wondered whether I was going to become addicted myself to the Ativan I was taking on a nightly basis. Would I ever be able to sleep without it?

That first night Mike was at Caron, we went to dinner with my godparents, Seva and Al. Seva is my mother's only biological sister, and we were staying with them for the night before heading back home to New York City. Seva and Al were both close to eighty years old. They had no children and were very simple people. They didn't spend all their money on Chanel bags and BMWs and expensive vacations. They lived in the same house forever, bought their clothes at the outlets, and drove matching cars. I worried about being alone with them now and talking about my son's addiction. What would they think? What would they say? How would I react if they didn't understand or tried to lecture me?

I felt like a fifty-year-old child walking down the hall to the principal's office. Oddly enough, my godfather had been a principal for many years before starting his law practice. With both my parents gone, I knew they would feel it was their duty to guide me through this mess, and I had to respect that because that's how I was raised. I was prepared for the worst.

I looked at my husband as he drove toward their house. The years had started to take their toll on me, but somehow he kept getting more handsome. His hair was getting grayer by the minute, but it looked sophisticated on him. Everyone and everything was changing. We were silent most of the time, but no words had to be spoken. We both knew how the other felt. I knew he was hurting. I knew he was questioning how this happened. I wanted to tell him that he was the greatest husband and father that ever lived, but I was too tired to speak. I'd lost the ability to do even that which came most naturally to me: take care of those around me.

As we pulled back into the driveway of my godparents' perfect little ranch in rural Pennsylvania, I felt a more terrifying fear than leaving my son behind: Would my children grow up to blame their problems on their mother?

At dinner my godparents verified how fortunate I was for my upbringing and how powerful a family's love can be. They were grateful to be close enough to see Mike on visitation days. They were happy we were staying with them since no one except my brother really visited them anymore. But most importantly, they did not condemn my son. Or us.

There were times I would look at my godmother and see my mother in her eyes. As I got older, we grew closer. She was one of the only people I felt safe around, and just like my mother, she knew how to cure anything with a hug.

But Al and I had never been very close. He was not a warm and fuzzy kind of guy when I was growing up. I hadn't seen him for a few years though, and when we'd arrived the night before, I noticed a change. Something about him was different. The night before we took Mike to treatment, he had spent a long time alone with Mike, talking with him just as a grandfather would.

It was a side of him I had never seen.

He told me I should be proud of my son because he wanted help. He pulled a newspaper clipping out from his pocket at dinner for me about how the former Miss America had gone through the substance abuse program at Caron, just as Mike was going to. This made him feel better knowing that Miss America got the help she needed from the same place Mike was at. I laughed to myself for the first time since setting out on this journey. It felt good to laugh for the first time in a long time.

I had decided I would not be visiting my son on the following Sunday, but my godparents were already planning to spend the afternoon with him. I gave them the list of the do's and don'ts, and watched as Al read it to my godmother. Their visit would take place one week into the program. My godmother insisted on sneaking cookies in somehow for all the boys in the program. My godfather shook his head at her, saying it wasn't allowed. As Michael and I sat across the table watching them argue about this, I knew he was thinking the same thing I was, because as tired as he was, he was listening to them and smiling.

That dinner could have been a night of finger pointing, uncomfortable questions, and lectures. But instead, two of the most revered people in my supersized Greek family were squabbling over what time they would need to leave home to be there on time, and how my son's great-aunt would smuggle cookies in to the boys in treatment. Michael felt the same relief I did. We knew my godfather would sit with Mike on Sunday and listen to him while my godmother rubbed his head and kissed him endlessly. It wasn't a burden. They were looking forward to it.

For the first time in days, I was grateful.

Once we got back to New York, I hoped everything would go back to normal. Everyone would fall back into a familiar, time-tested routine of pretending everything was OK.

Everyone except for me.

Mike

I remember being admitted and feeling a sense of joy. Detox hadn't kicked in yet, and I still felt happy. I actually felt happy to be there. Once I had been left alone, my future started to look a little brighter for the first time in a long time. I remember being brought up to the unit in a van by a guy named Joe. The unit was comparable to a college dorm. It was where I would be for the next thirty days at Caron. I wasn't feeling any other emotions at that point because they had been tucked so far underneath from drugs. There weren't any feelings of shame, guilt, or fear yet. But that would come soon.

The first week was simple as I ran through the motions of whatever was thrown my way. I wasn't defiant toward the groups and activities. I was willing to take direction at that point. I saw others getting angry or sad, yelling, or crying, but I just sat there, still just an empty shell. Looking back, I may have easily been diagnosed as a sociopath.

That second week, I started feeling—barely. But the roller coaster had only just begun. Loneliness and fear were the primary feelings. I was afraid of what was to come when I left this place. I was surrounded by twenty or thirty other guys and I was beginning to have cravings again for a fix to drown the feelings of fear I was having. I would think of getting something, *anything*, to calm my nerves, and a physical chill would go down my spine. The sensation was so strong that I would almost feel that sense of ease and comfort that my medicine brought me.

Even if for only a moment. I had fear that I would never be free of this craving and obsession. I knew that it was possible to be sober but didn't think I could be happy and sober at the same time. At that point, my fear and shame were just combining into pure anger. I can remember not wanting to go to groups anymore, the gym, or even go eat with the unit. I just wanted to be by myself and sleep the pain away.

That particular Friday there was a group of young men from a halfway house that came to speak from Lancaster, Pennsylvania. Something one of the speakers said that night started to give me hope. His words made me feel not so alone. He spoke of growing up and feeling insecure and out of place and different from everyone else. He said he had always had a void in his heart that he could never fill and that he constantly tried to fill that void with alcohol and drugs. This man stood there and said everything that I had always felt. These were things that took me to the place of using drugs, yet he stood before me sober, proud, and happy. I no longer felt alone in this world and knew there was hope to live a life without drugs.

Insecurities, low self-esteem, self-consciousness, no self-worth! A whole lot of *self*. This is what I had concerned myself with my entire life. How people viewed me. How could I be the cool guy that everyone would look at and say, "I want what that guy has"? I then began to set myself on a cycle in which I could achieve this by any means necessary, mainly driven by lies, manipulation, and pure selfishness, although at the time I didn't think I was doing anything wrong. I had always felt lower than others, like I had something to prove to them. It seemed like everyone was always making fun of me behind my back, and my thoughts about myself would manifest as real. I would tell myself that I was a nobody and a loser. I would tell myself that I was worthless, that I was nothing. So I became a people pleaser, doing things and serving others thinking I was being a good person, but I always had selfish intentions. These acts of pleasing others were only to build myself up as a person in their eyes so that I could tell myself I was worth it. I began to build my ego.

I remember being young. Really young. One of my "friends" whose approval I was probably still trying to gain was over at our house. We were up late, and I had the great idea of breaking into my parents' liquor cabinet. We would then begin to try every type of booze there was. We got drunk and had that drunken bonding experience that goes on, where you tell each other how cool the other is. Suddenly something happened where I had the step up on others. Other than the booze taking my fear of judgment from me, I felt like I was wanted, even *needed* for something. Word had spread that I was that cool kid who drank.

This pattern progressed even further throughout my life. Once others started drinking and it became more normal, I had to think of how else I could get people to need me. So as I began to smoke pot, others needed me to get it for them. I was needed once again. Not only were weed and alcohol covering up my feelings about myself, they also made me a necessity for others.

I continued to experiment and drink and smoke pot in high school. Following the same progression, I got into coke and mushrooms. However, when I found opiates, I knew that that was all I wanted to do. They were all I would ever need. Drinking had never really been my thing. When I drank, I drank a lot, but once I found opiates, I didn't need to drink so much anymore.

Drinking didn't work; it was never a problem for me. Maybe it would have been if I hadn't had the opiates—I'm not sure.

I had undergone surgery my freshman year of high school due to an injury while playing lacrosse. I had torn my labrum and had surgery on my shoulder. They had given me a prescription of Percocet. I knew nothing about abusing painkillers.

Some of the upperclassmen—once they found out about my surgery—asked for some of my Percocet. I stepped back, and before I handed any over, I asked what this was all about. I was curious to know why they wanted them. That was when I started taking over the prescribed dosage and suddenly felt like life and everything else was going to be OK and better than I ever expected. My insecurity, fear, guilt, and pain started to feel as if they had been freed from me, when actually they were just being tucked away. I found my one true love, one that made me not care about what other people thought of me and made everything all right. I could talk to anyone with confidence, especially women. I felt like the funny guy, and mostly I just felt on top of the world.

During the month at Caron, we had to make a time-line of drug usage, and I could easily see that at certain points when weed and alcohol were at an all-time high, opiates were almost out of the picture for me. But when opiates were at an all-time high, the other stuff was out of the picture. This is when I began to realize that I always needed something in me to help me feel the way I wanted to feel. I didn't want to be me because I was afraid of who that was.

CHAPTER 3

I JUST WANTED TO BE ME, IF ONLY FOR A MOMENT

Anita

I grew up in Pawtucket, Rhode Island, and my family lived there until I entered ninth grade. My father, being a priest, was the reason we lived in a massive colonial mansion that was the parish house. The house was so huge that I used to ride my bicycle on the first floor. I loved our house. The safety and warmth of those memories is something I always wanted to pass along to my own children. Every memory I have of my childhood was wonderful, and I can say that in all honesty.

But when I was in eighth grade, our archbishop told my father we were relocating to the cathedral in New York City and I was crushed. I did everything in my power to try and prevent it from happening. I even sent

41

a petition signed by hundreds of kids in my school to the archbishop with the reasons why we shouldn't move. Unlike my brother (who was the perfect child), I was a major troublemaker, true to the saying "priest's daughter, devil's granddaughter."

I'd exhausted myself trying to keep us from moving, but it was my father's doctors who had the final say. They didn't want him to move to New York City because of a heart attack he had suffered a few years earlier.

I was very relieved. I was also very naïve.

Before I could celebrate, we were packing and on our way to Rye, New York to be closer to the archbishop. The doctor's concerns had merely kept us from living in Manhattan. We were still moving. The archbishop wanted my father close to him so we were moving no matter what.

Being a Greek Orthodox priest meant that you could be married as long as it was before you were ordained as a priest. My father would have to deal with a huge community of people and try to keep everybody happy. It was the same as being in politics. Actually it's exactly the same. Luckily my father had my mother behind him. Any priest's kid (a.k.a. PK) will tell you that our mothers are saints. My mother would break her back entertaining kings and queens from Greece, politicians, bishops, archbishops, and anyone else that came to visit. I can remember being eight years old and having to squeeze bags of fresh oranges for certain visitors that requested it. My mother would bake and bake for days, making all of the famous Greek pastries to entertain visitors. Then she would cook and cook all the holiday favorites, such as pastitso and lamb, and roll hundreds of stuffed grape leaves just for people who would come over after church services. Then she would do it all over again for the family. She never stopped. She never stopped helping my father build up the churches and the communities. She was the glue that held our family together. She was the glue that held my father together, who held the church together.

I started high school in 1974, which was the year we moved to Rye. We lived next door to my father's church, and I went to the Catholic all-girls' high school right next door on the other side of the church. School of the Holy Child. It's a rude awakening when your father is a priest and you are thrown in with girls from families of excessive wealth. I knew I had to lose my New England accent as fast as possible and try to fit in. I ended up making friends pretty quickly and have remained very close to some of those friends, one of them being my best friend, Joanie.

Joanie would ride her horse to my house back then, and we spent a lot of time together. We've been through a lot together and have always been there for one another, no matter how far away we physically are. We've been friends for over forty years now. My daughter gave her the nickname Trigger because whenever one of us has a problem, we sit down in front of a good chick flick and polish off a five-pound bag of M&Ms together. Although we are in our fifties, I still feel like I'm in high school whenever we're together. I trust her with my deepest thoughts, and she has carefully guided me through much of the situation I was facing with my son. If I am unsure of making a decision, I know that she will help me decide which path to choose.

In 1978, after I had graduated high school, I was getting ready to leave for Greece to attend the American University in Athens. My uncle Spiro, who was my father's brother, was married and had no children, so he made me an offer I couldn't refuse. He offered me an apartment in Athens and my own car to drive while I went to school there. I was so excited and couldn't wait to start packing for this amazing experience. As luck would have it, two weeks before leaving, my father told me plans had changed because of some political problems happening in Greece.

"It's just not a good idea right now," he explained. "It's not safe."

I was furious. There was no time to apply anywhere else, as most schools were starting in two weeks. Even though I knew it wasn't what I wanted to do with my life, I enrolled at a local college for Fashion Marketing and Management. The day I graduated, in 1980, I answered an ad for a job at a Park Avenue advertising agency.

I was assigned to a creative team and got my first taste of television production. I worked for eight different producers and fell in love with the excitement of taking a concept into reality. It was fun and fast paced and brought out a side of me I never knew existed. I started working closely with the head of casting, and when she moved on to another agency, I was given her job. I always considered myself a good judge of character, and casting came naturally. I was able to see people for what they could be, not necessarily what they were.

This was back in the days of Studio 54, and I had access to A-list parties every night of the week. I would have invitations and free passes stacked on my desk and went to as many events as I could. I didn't want to miss out on any of it. When I was out too late to take the train back to Rye, which was most nights, I crashed on Kathy's couch. She had been a close friend since high school and had just gotten a great apartment in midtown. I would have to entertain the hot male models for work and Kathy was the perfect person to do that with. It didn't matter that they were mostly hot gay men as long as we could dance all night and get the job done the next day.

Kathy and all my other girlfriends had amazing jobs and the city was our playground. Michael and I had just started dating, and we felt like we owned the city. It was perfect.

Michael came from a very close Catholic family, so I held off telling him that my father was a Greek Orthodox priest. I held off from letting my own father know how serious my relationship was getting with a Catholic as

45

well. We had been attending one of Michael's family parties one night when I finally allowed him to drive me home. I couldn't put it off any longer. It was dark, and I knew he wouldn't be able to see the church next to my house. In between the church and our family home, which was very modest, was the massive Tudor mansion that housed all of the offices and classrooms for the church. It was at the front door of this house that I had Michael drop me off that night. When he returned to his family party, he burst in exclaiming, "I don't know what her father does for a living, but she's loaded!" Poor guy had no idea how wrong he was.

When I finally told him the truth, he in turn told his mother that I was not Catholic. All he could say to her in his defense was, "But mom, you always wanted to have a priest in the family!" The next thing I knew, we were planning a big fat Greek/Irish wedding. Between our two families and the size of my father's congregation, we ended up having over four hundred people for the big day. Including the service and the reception, we ended up having a celebration that lasted for ten hours.

Our wedding took place in May 1984, and we went to Greece for our honeymoon. As soon as we returned, Michael immediately started working on building a successful career on Wall Street. Back then, brokers entertained their clients with front row tickets to every concert and Broadway show. They took limousines, ate fancy dinners, and pretty much did anything and everything to impress the client.

Michael never took advantage of any of his brokers by asking for himself, but I did. I abused every privilege I could, but I always took care of those guys right back. At least three or four times a week, one of my husband's broker friends would call me for club passes to model parties. They would have big clients to entertain and getting them into the exclusive clubs and private parties were like golden tickets. I would get them whatever they wanted, sending the passes over to their offices by bike messenger.

We had a great racket going. We were young and wild and living the life.

Then I got pregnant.

Halfway through my pregnancy, we bought our first house in Rye, and as a young couple just starting out, we dumped our savings into the house and did all the work ourselves. I would be waddling around, painting every room of the house, and loving every minute of it.

At the time there wasn't even a choice. I went from a badass working girl who treated Manhattan like her own personal playground to a barefoot and pregnant housewife decorating her house in the suburbs, faster than the Metro North gets you to Grand Central.

It was a big change but something I looked forward to. I'd always known I wanted a family and was ready for the adventure. I also knew I'd have my mother to rely on if there was anything I couldn't handle. She always took care of everything and everyone, and was better than any parenting book.

But when I was twenty-nine, my mother was diagnosed with breast cancer.

I thought I was the one that was going to die. I had been bugging her for two years to go to the doctor because of a lump that she had shown me. She was stubborn though. I had to trick her into seeing my pediatrician while at my daughter Alex's appointment. My mother loved my pediatrician and I had him call her in from the waiting room to hold Alex while she was vaccinated.

"I need to see what your daughter told me about," he said. She eventually let him check her and recommended a specialist for her.

The illness lasted for six years. Toward the end, she lived with us between treatments and being in and out of the hospital. It involved doing physical things that only a daughter could do.

My main concern was my mother's dignity through all of this. I didn't want my brother or father to see the ugliness of her cancer. I would always make sure she had pedicures and manicures and facials, and I would try to do her makeup and hair perfectly every day. In between the bouts of chemo, she would get her appetite back and would request all kinds of crazy stuff like lobster and bubble gum. My girlfriends would all take turns cooking and bringing over dinner just to help out.

My daughter Alex was so close to her *yiayia* but was still too young to understand how sick she was. She would sit with her in our den and make my mother watch the movie *Beaches* over and over and over again. If my mother would need to get up and I wasn't in the room, our yellow lab, Winston, who was always sprawled out on the floor at my mother's feet, would spring into action. He would stand in front of my mother as she put her hands on his strong back to hoist herself up. He would follow her into whatever room she would go to and again plop down at her feet. Winston was the world's best nurse.

The night before she passed, her Hospice caregiver, a beautiful Jamaican woman, called us to my parent's house to talk to us. She said my grandparents, who were both deceased, had been to see my mother during the night. Her description of them was so vivid and precise that no one could be skeptical of her story.

"They watched over your mother's bed all night," she said. She then explained that we needed to call in the family, as this meant she was going to pass. My cousin Dionne flew in right away from Chicago, and we sat by my mother's bedside as my brother calmly stroked her face and read from the Bible. Then, just like that, she took her last breath.

I lost my best friend. Just like that, she was gone.

We had always had a summer home on Cape Cod, which is where most of my mother's family lived. When my mother passed, I decided to stay there full time just to be surrounded by my family. We still had our house in Rye, and Michael would go back and forth on the weekends while still working in New York City. It was something I felt I needed to do to avoid a nervous breakdown when my mother passed. I look back now and regret having done it. I never should have left my husband or my father, but I did. I never should have taken my children away from their roots, but I did. I just wanted to get away from the pain of my loss and be where I had happy memories of my mother. Staying put and seeing a therapist would have been a better option at the time.

That wrong decision has taught me more than anything else has in life. I've learned that you can't move forward while holding on to mistakes from the past. So I leave that mistake in the same place I keep the people who still talk about it behind my back—behind me.

A few years after moving to the cape full time, my father was diagnosed with Alzheimer's.

Seeing my father behave the way he did after all those years of being a priest was difficult. My poor brother would get so upset with his behavior that I started worrying about him as well. My brother was all I had. It was just the two of us, and I couldn't let anything happen to him.

We finally had to put my dad into an assisted living facility near my brother so he could take care of him. Watching your parent revert back to being a child is frightening. I think this disease was worse than the cancer because there was no way of knowing what would happen next as this disease progressed. Either way, I lost my parents way too young and wish I still had them. They were two people who always knew what to do. I never gave my father credit for that. I only realize now that he was right about a lot of things. I wish I had listened to him while I still had him.

If anyone had asked me where I would be at fifty, I would have told them that my kids would be off and running their own lives and Michael and I would be island-hopping around Greece on our private yacht.

But in 2009, there was no yacht and no island. To make matters worse, my family's life together was starting to change. Alex had graduated from Emerson College in Boston and moved out to Los Angeles. She was going out there to chase her dream of working in the entertainment industry, and Mike was just finishing up his second year at UVM.

We were still living on Cape Cod, but with each day it felt less like home. After sending furniture off to LA for Alex's new apartment and to Vermont for the house Mike was sharing with some of his friends, my nest was empty.

Michael had lost his job in Boston at Bear Stearns, which shut down altogether soon after, and when the real estate industry crashed as well, we had to live off our retirement savings. I went from selling five to six houses a year to selling none.

Everything was different. We started to downsize our lives little by little. Cars were traded in, gardeners were let go, the pool was shut down, and the previously endless line of friends coming over every night to eat our food and drink our wine came to a screeching halt.

Our house was the one where everyone came to gather, but once we prepared to sell and there were decks to be repaired, rooms to be painted, and staircases to rebuild, our "friends" were nowhere to be found. If not for a few who cared, who showed up day after day to help my poor husband with the repairs, none of it would have gotten done.

Life as we knew it was changing, and it was changing fast.

As we started letting go of the past, my new best friend was the delete button on my phone.

During all this turmoil, my husband never complained. Other than the time he smashed his toe with a hammer trying to fix the deck, he never made a peep.

His silence made it even more heartbreaking when we had to sell his boat. It was a simple, fun little boat, but he loved taking the kids out or going out for the day with his friends. And now it was gone. Losing something that had become a part of our family's traditions made everything real. Never again would we pile on with all the cousins and cruise around Nantucket Sound.

Although I loved Cape Cod, I was ready for some stimulation. With Michael getting a new job in the city, everyone in my family had something new and exciting to look forward to. Everyone, that is, but me. I didn't know what I was going to do, but I knew that I had to work because we were flat broke, and the burden could not be on my husband alone.

When we first moved to New York, my cousin Nikolas, who was a new agent in my real estate office back on Cape Cod, took over selling the house at the industry's lowest point in years. He listed our house and started to pursue buyers. The market was tanking and short sales and foreclosures were blazing a new trail across the cape. I tried to keep his spirits up by telling him how it could only get better.

At the time, I didn't realize I was lying.

It never crossed my mind that we would get anything less than the asking price on our home. It had been our home for eighteen years and was a private little oasis. It was so hidden away that people would call it "a secret." We thought it would sell quickly. From my years in the business, I knew it was a great house. Only a few years earlier, it would have sold before the ink had dried on the contracts. It was our big retirement investment. At least that's what we thought.

A week on the market turned into two, two weeks turned into months, and months turned into a year. All the while, we had to carry that house while living in New York City.

We had always looked at the house as the second part of our retirement fund. It killed me to admit we would need to lower the price in order to make a sale, but we had no choice. New York City was where my husband's new job was, so we needed to make a sale and move on. Unfortunately, so many people had second homes on the cape, and when the financial crisis hit, these were the first things that people tried to sell. They were giving away their homes just to get rid of them, which lowered the value of ours. After some debate, we decided to drastically reduce the asking price and head for New York.

We took enough furniture for a two-bedroom apartment and put the rest into storage. I've always been surrounded by my family photos, and my mother's and grandmother's things, and I didn't really understand how much comfort they had provided until I had to pack up my memories and put them in a cold, empty storage facility. The seemingly simple act really messed with my head.

I felt like I didn't have a home any more. And I'm sure, in some way, my kids felt the same way. Our feelings would have to wait though, as the more pressing concern was how I was going to find a job in New York City at the age of forty-nine.

The first thing I did was pick up the phone and call Louise, a high school friend who was a very successful realtor in the city. I had been doing real estate for years and figured it was a safer bet than starting over in something new. As much as I loathed catering to buyers and sellers, I figured with everything else in my world flipped on its ear, maybe I would just look for something familiar. Something easy.

When I enrolled in classes for my New York State realtor's license, I couldn't believe how packed the classes were. I was surrounded by college grads with MBA's taking a real estate course because they couldn't find a job. It wasn't just my life that was changing—the whole world was changing. And it sucked. I felt really old.

As much as I missed seeing my daughter on a regular basis, I was grateful she had a job and some security in her life after college. She wasn't sitting in a room like this, her eyes filled with the fear and uncertainty I saw in the kids next to me.

I finished my course, passed the test, and called Louise. She set me up with an interview at a big Manhattan real estate company, and I felt very fortunate to be hired for their new boutique office on Madison Avenue.

Nothing in my years of Cape Cod real estate experience and nothing I'd learned in the New York State classes could have prepared me for the culture shock of joining this Madison Avenue real estate office. I had a built-in client base on the cape but had to start from scratch in New York. It was humbling to be starting at the bottom after feeling like a big fish in a small pond for so many years. Walking into my first office meeting was like walking into a debutante ball: the fur coats hanging carelessly over the back of nearly every chair, the designer clothes and extravagant jewelry everyone wore every day, the full makeup and professionally done hair, no khakis or topsiders in sight. I would have been nervous even if they had been friendly, but no one said hello or even so much as acknowledged my presence. I felt like a new kid from out of town on the first day of school. It was ninth grade all over again.

Before even leaving the office, I'd been stripped down to nothing. It wasn't the confidence boost I needed before tackling the streets of New York City.

Because of the "cost of doing business," people were cutthroat in the city. Every project had to be a big secret; otherwise, it could be snatched away by a so-called coworker.

I could not see spending my days with these people. They were the epitome of everything I'd steered clear of my entire life. Even with the near-constant contact I had with people, and women my own age, I began to feel more and more lonely.

I was at a very strange, confusing stage of my life. I thought to myself, "Why am I trying to continue on that same path selling real estate?" Because I thought it would be easy. Because I had been scared. And real estate had felt safe.

It was right around this time that suddenly I found myself thinking about death a lot. I lost my parents at young ages, and I started waking up in the middle of the night, thinking about how much time I had left in life. I found myself organizing everything and anything I could get my hands on in case something happened to me. Color coding files and showing my husband where everything was in the "files of our lives." I was panicked about the uncertainty of life. I felt as if I were hiding behind a dark, heavy curtain, peeking out waiting for something bad to happen. I was worried about my son. I wondered who would help him if something happened to me. I was missing my daughter terribly, and I was scared, worried, and filled with angst every single moment of every single day.

My saving grace was taking our bloodhound, Skilo, for long walks in Central Park. (Skilo is the Greek word for dog) Twice a day I would throw on some sneakers and grab her leash, feeling just as excited as she was to get outside. During these times I would try to clear my head and figure out what I, the mother who had lost her identity, was going to do next. I wanted to do something that mattered. I wanted to do something that I would love doing so I could pour my heart into it.

My identity, much like many women's, had gone from being a daughter to a wife to a mother. But now, some thirty years later, who was I? My friend Nancy once told me, "I'm somewhere between fifty and dead." And that's how I felt. Stuck right in the middle of two options I wasn't ready for. I wanted to be something more.

I wasn't sure what I wanted to do, but I was very sure that real estate wasn't it. And if I could go at any moment, I wasn't about to waste any more time on something that didn't make me happy.

I wanted to be just me, if only for a moment.

CHAPTER 4

HEART ATTACKS ARE FOR BOYS

Anita

In the fall of 2009, Mike had called us from school and told us that he was addicted to pain pills and needed help. He had been living in Vermont that previous summer and had been working for an environmental company. He had been seeing a therapist because of his so-called depression, whom he had given permission to speak to us, and we decided that although he was trying to get off these things himself, he needed help. We pulled him out of school on a medical emergency, and he came to live with us in New York. I had friends who had been down this path with their own kids before, so I started reaching out for help.

I called psychiatrists, therapists, addiction centers, inpatient programs, and outpatient programs and started compiling information about what to do. The only thing I knew was that insurance wasn't going to cover anything.

Luckily for me, my cousin is a therapist in New York. She recommended a psychologist for Mike, who, after meeting with us, decided it would be best to get him into an outpatient program at a hospital. This doctor was the first person to give me a glimmer of hope. He listened and seemed to actually care about what happened to us after we left his office.

I had Mike see a famous hypnotherapist, hired a trainer to help him get his body healthy, and sent him for acupuncture to try and eliminate the crap that was in his body. Mike had had three surgeries back to back from lacrosse injuries on both shoulders and his left ankle. I thought this could help get rid of any leftover pain he was experiencing. Pain, which could have been contributing to his continued pill usage.

He was miserable. He was moody and distant, and it was an awful summer for all of us. Mike was turning into someone I didn't recognize. He kept assuring me that it was him trying to stay away from drugs on his own.

"I'll get through it," he assured me. "I can do this on my own."

Both my husband and I were in denial. We didn't realize how serious the problem was. We thought he was depressed.

Mike went back to school that spring and came to live with us for the summer in New York City.

I had him see a highly recommended psychologist that summer. One of the reasons I didn't think he was on drugs at that point was that the doctor told my husband and I that we needed to stop putting so much pressure on our son. If we eased off, he would be fine. He lectured us on how parents today pile pressure on their kids to succeed and to push them to be who *we want them to be.*

That stupid asshole.

I had to hold myself back from slapping that idiot in the face. But my son had fooled him as well. This guy couldn't even tell that Mike was high as a kite while sitting right in front of him. I didn't find any of this out until going through family treatment while Mike was at Caron.

For a brief moment, I listened to a friend of mine when she told me to stop focusing on my son and figure out what I wanted to do in life. She told me to focus on myself and on something positive for a change. Since she was single and had no children, it was easy for her to say this, but I'm thankful that I did listen to her long enough to follow her advice.

It was difficult to figure out just exactly who I should have been taking advice from. Everyone had an opinion. There would be friends who were in such denial about their own kids that obviously I couldn't listen to them. I was past the denial phase. There were my friends who always wanted to meet for a drink to talk about what to do for my son—any excuse to meet for a drink. I couldn't listen to them either. Little by little I started to realize that everywhere I looked, many of my own friends had their own addiction issues. I couldn't rely on any of them to advise me, so I concentrated on reaching out to people who had faced the battle head on for either themselves or for their children. I started surrounding myself with a whole new support group. That was the best decision I could have made.

When I decided to walk away from the mundane world of real estate, some of my friends I had worked with on the cape gave me a hard time about not trying to make it in the city. "I guess you can't make it anywhere," a friend cackled into the phone from hundreds of miles away.

I had to laugh about it because he was so clueless. He wouldn't have been able to even figure out how to get to the subway to get to the office meetings. It was very simple back there, and if it had been the same here, I probably would have kept doing it. In many ways I'm thankful it wasn't. I had to keep searching for a passion.

Going for a walk was something I never did living on the Cape. I drove everywhere, and we had a large backyard, so I would just let Skilo out to run around alone. In the city we had to explore together, armed with a leash and poop bags. I can remember the day I started paying attention to everything happening in Central Park and on the streets around me. There were dogs and dog walkers everywhere. I've always been an animal freak, especially for dogs, and have always wanted to do something where I could work with animals. It just never seemed like a "career." Who knew that my career path of my youth would find its way into my future?

Since having Alex in 1987, I hadn't thought about getting back into the entertainment industry. Even after working on a movie in 2007 with my friend Michael, who owned a New York–based production company, I was still content to sell houses and raise my family.

But now I wanted to work in television. After years out of the entertainment world I couldn't just dive into television and pick out a new career like a pair of shoes. I needed to start somewhere. And that's why I went to work for my friend Michael at his production company. (Because of all the other Michaels in my life, I just called this one Mailer.)

He knew what I was capable of doing and had given me the nickname the Fixer. I had been hired to do some casting work for a movie and received a co-producer credit because I ended up getting so involved. I never had a problem fixing anything for someone else, and with a nickname like that, I was furious I couldn't fix my son.

I knew Mailer would let me come work with him. I just hadn't known it was what I wanted to do.

Knowing I didn't want to be cooped up for too long, I wasted little time before approaching him about an idea I had for a show about New York City dog walkers.

It was like a doggie soap opera. I said to Mailer, "I want to show how they become part of our families and show the rescue work they do alongside of it. If the show does well, we can give back to shelters." I knew that I had found something I could do, make money at, and give back all at the same time. He agreed that it was a great idea so we decided to do it together.

Once finished, we chose an agent to represent the show. Waiting has never been my strong suit, and now I had to fight off the anxiety, doubt, and fear of putting myself out there.

Immediately a major network wanted to talk to us. They were interested in our dog reality show. It was really exciting for me because it was my first meeting at a network, and I was excited to pitch and talk about my ideas. Days before the meeting I kept having these strange pains in my cheeks, and I assumed I had been grinding my teeth at night due to nerves about the pitch. I just ignored it, hoping it would go away. I was praying it wasn't related to the stress my son had brought on. All the worry, all the stress…was it manifesting itself in my face? I was afraid that it was something bad, but I wouldn't face it. I just prayed it would go away.

The network decided to film a pilot and five episodes. It all happened so fast—I couldn't believe it. I left that office and went over to meet my husband at an outside restaurant to celebrate. I can remember Michael's friend Steve asking me why my face was so red, and I attributed it to the fact that my cheekbones were throbbing with pain still. I also thought that it would go away now that we had received such great news. It was one of the happiest days of my life, and I was really proud of what I had accomplished. Too bad my son showed up to meet us and was a moody little miserable prick. He totally ruined my day once again, and I totally once again ignored the fact that he was slipping away into this person I did not recognize.

I was mad at him, excited for the show, and afraid of what the pain was in my face all at the same time.

Within a few weeks, the pain in my cheeks was so bad that one night my husband had to take me to the emergency room.

The only place I had pain was in my face, but it was the worst pain I'd ever experienced. I can remember being in the cab on our way to the emergency room, looking at my husband, who was petrified. He had a look of terror on his face. I asked him if he was worried because he wouldn't be able to find his dry cleaning tickets if I died. I can still hear the cabbie laughing at this as he dropped us off at the hospital.

They set me up with a cardiologist the next morning. He was supposedly one of the best in New York City. He sent me home with a prescription for antibiotics, telling me I had an infection in my tooth. I knew he was wrong, but I played along because it made me feel better and I didn't want anyone to worry. I didn't want to worry. I had to stay focused on my son.

Two weeks later we were at our cape house—that wouldn't sell—for the Fourth of July. I was cooking breakfast for my son and a bunch of his friends when the pain returned tenfold and shot down to my shoulders and across my chest. My son's friend was sitting at the counter telling me about law school. As he spoke, his voice was getting more and more faint. I stood frozen with fear while watching the bacon sizzle and burn as if in slow motion. I was thinking to myself, "Wouldn't this be the appropriate way for me to die? Cooking?"

At Cape Cod Hospital, I was in the ER, and a young cardiologist, Dr. Peter, came in and said I'd be staying a few days for testing. He was certain I had experienced a heart attack. I assured him it was just an infection in my tooth, according to the brilliant cardiologist in New York, but he was not letting me leave. Once I found out he was Greek, I trusted him, and as I lay there hooked up to all the crazy machines, I quizzed him about his dating status. We've been best friends since.

Once they had proof of a blockage, they scheduled my stent procedure, which you have to stay awake for to give permission to place the stent where necessary. They wheeled me in and asked if I'd like some classical music playing while they did the procedure. I demanded Aerosmith, and they obliged. I was surrounded by lots of different people—nurses, aides, surgeons—and I decided to create a makeshift reality show called *Stent This*. I cast each and every one of them, and we played out a few scenes. I could feel the stinging glare of my cardiologist behind the glass partition when he arrived and saw what was happening. Apparently it was a serious procedure, and he didn't appreciate me making a game of it.

The next few days in the hospital, everything hit me. I had this crazy epiphany, and I couldn't stop crying when I realized that I actually could have died. My husband and son were with me the whole time, and I could tell my son was filled with fear. I remember thinking to myself that he would get his act together seeing me like this. I couldn't have been more wrong.

When I was alone at night in that hospital, I reflected on my life and all the things I had done wrong. I had made so many mistakes and had taken so much for granted that I couldn't wait to get out of there and make up for all the times I had treated my husband like crap. Why did it take something this dire to make me realize what I'd known all along? That I was married to the greatest, kindest, most selfless man on earth. That was my goal for however many years I had left in life—to be the best wife I could be.

I also decided nothing was going to stand in the way of my own life goals. It was as if a light went off in my head, showing me that I was not too old to create and write and do all those things I never did while raising a family. I had just turned fifty. My father and brother both had heart attacks at fifty. I never for a minute thought it would happen to me. I had been waiting for my mother's breast cancer to find me.

Not a heart attack! Those are for boys!

Everyone's always talking about how fifty is the new twenty-five, blah, blah, blah. What a bunch of crap. Heart attack or not, it's when you realize what and who matters in life. It's also a time of doing all the things you've always wanted to do but were afraid to try.

I finally went home to sleep in my own bed and woke the next morning to my beautiful daughter standing over me. She was staring at me like I might disappear if she looked away. She had flown in from Los Angeles, and I couldn't have been happier to see her. It was just what I needed, some alone time with my little girl. We all decided that my husband and son would head back to New York to work, and Alex would stay to take care of me.

I had just come home from the hospital, and some close friends had come over to visit. Michael was out front packing up the car when out of the blue, Mike started throwing a fit. He just exploded into this crazed rage, screaming that he should stay too. It was the last thing I needed.

He had been so strange and acting like such an ass that I honestly didn't want him around. He couldn't care less about upsetting me. That crushed me. It made me hate him. Yes, I admit it. I hated my son. All I wanted was for him to go away. How foolish I was in the hospital, thinking that seeing me that way would make him change. I realized right then and there that all he cared about was himself. If I had only known then what I know now about addiction. It wasn't my son. It was the drugs. I had to give in to the fact that no matter what we did to try and help him, none of it mattered until he wanted the help himself.

I would make excuses for Mike, saying he just wanted to stay and help me. I always made excuses for him. I knew it was a lie. He just wanted to stay and hang out with his friends, and I wanted him off Cape Cod for good. I couldn't wait for the damn house to sell so he would not be able to go there whenever he wanted. He had a few good friends, but there were so many "problem" friends that I hated it when he was there. I never considered the possibility that he was the problem. I never really looked at my son. I just seemed to always look past him and blame everyone else for who he had become.

I sat in bed that night, unable to go to sleep. I was afraid. Not for my heart, or my health, but because of how I felt about my own son. I was a mother. How could I be capable of such hatred?

How could I make it go away?

His behavior that day I came home after my heart attack, and the ugliness I saw in him, made me want to take my friend's advice though. I wanted to focus on myself. I just didn't know how to without having the guilt of not focusing on him.

Mike

In the summer of 2010, certain events were happening. My mom had experienced a heart attack, and we were selling our family home, but even at that point, I continued to make everything all about me. A normal person would show love and care toward his family, but I drowned myself in drugs and self-pity. I made myself out to be the victim. I acted as if I was the only one affected by this whole mess.

I was living at my parents' apartment that summer and working for my mother's friend Tim at a women's clothing store. Selling bargain designer clothing to women was not my specialty, and it became very hard for me to be helpful and keep a smile on my face without help. Most days, the only way that I could handle doing that job was by driving to Rye to get enough cocaine to get me through the shift. It wasn't my first choice of drug, but it would help me be social and courteous to customers. It also gave me an excuse to make frequent trips to the bathroom.

My craving for pills had such a hold on me that there were times I would say I was taking the car to Rye for the day to hang out with friends, but in reality I would drive three and a half hours all the way back to Cape Cod just to grab pills from someone I knew. I knew I could probably find stuff in the city but couldn't risk the chance that I may not find anything. Driving eight hours round trip didn't seem like such a bad idea when I knew I could get what I was looking for at a good price. Most of the time, I would spend my whole paycheck and buy enough to last me the week.

I would tell myself, "OK. I have twenty pills. I could limit it to two a day, maybe two and a half some days, and I'll be fine until next week."

But my craving was never sated after the first one or two. The entire batch would only last me until lunchtime of the following day. It always seemed worth it until the batch was gone.

At the end of the summer, my parents asked me if I would go see a therapist while I was contemplating joining the Coast Guard. I told myself, "Sure. Why not?" After all, it was an opportunity to try and get a professional on my side, someone who my parents confided in. Someone who could help me get them off my back. For my first session, I brought a bag of cocaine and a handful of Percocet.

I was so loaded and in my own world that I believed my own lies. Since my delusion was true to me, it appeared true to him, so in some ways I manipulated this man into buying into my self-pity and role as a victim. I could have won an Oscar that day. As soon as I was in his office, I began to bawl my eyes out. I think the tears covered up how high I was.

"I never wanted to go to that school! I wanted to go to Springfield and play lacrosse, but my parents wouldn't let me!

"My parents put so much pressure on me to do well in school and to finish that I can't take it!

"I can't even make my own decisions because my parents are so controlling!"

It was all me, me, me, me, and me. The performance worked. The therapist told me I should just concern myself with going back up to Vermont and getting space from my parents and that he "will handle them."

CHAPTER 5

WORST CHRISTMAS EVER

Anita

When Mike went back to school for his senior year, our house had still not sold on the cape, and it was becoming impossible to keep up with the bills. We ended up selling the house for much less than we owed on it and took out a private loan to pay off the rest. In short, we are still paying for a house that we don't own anymore.

In the meantime, Mike was constantly calling to ask for money. He told us he loved skiing and being healthy. I, of course, was sending him whatever I had because I just wanted him to stay away from drugs. I also felt bad for him because he seemed to always be getting tickets and flat tires, having his car towed, buying more schoolbooks, and everything else under the sun, for which I would send him money. I thought I was being a good mother. I was a stupid mother.

Michael and I had gone up to visit in Vermont, and Mike was constantly disappearing while we were there. His behavior was weird to say the least. Always on his phone, always saying, "Be right back." I thought he was dating a girl he didn't want us to meet. Little did I know he was dealing drugs.

Was I so wrapped up in my own life? Was the fact that I was going to sell my first TV show standing in the way of my seeing what was happening to my son? Was I pissed that it seemed to finally be about my husband and me getting some financial relief that I didn't have time to focus on anything other than making that happen? Was I just so stupid to think that as long as I cleaned his clothes and made home-cooked meals and tidied up his room that it would all be OK? That when we left Vermont and headed back to New York City, he would be OK because of my organizing his stuff? I was in full-blown denial because I actually think I chose to be.

Mike

After continuing to see the therapist for the rest of the summer, I had taken his advice and returned back to Vermont to continue school. He only believed it was the right decision because I told him I was sober the whole time during the previous semester. In reality, I was loaded 90 percent of the time.

I felt this time I could really do it on my own. This time would be different.

Once I was back in Vermont, I was taking three classes and started working at a restaurant washing dishes. I even picked up a painting gig working on the exterior of houses. I believed this made me responsible. Who cared if I was doing some drugs and drinking on the side? I barely had time for it anyway.

My parents were happy because I was in school, and others viewed me as a responsible workhorse. It never occurred to me I was still doing these things for all the wrong reasons: to make others happy, create another ego or identity for myself, and to feel like I had a purpose and was needed.

The same cycle began—or continued—that ran my life all through high school. I wasn't good enough, so I needed to prove myself.

Before too long, the guilt and shame crept back in. I still didn't feel like I knew who I was, or that enough people cared about me. I mean, when I played lacrosse, I felt like I was somebody. I was part of something. But that was behind me.

At that point I was making a good amount of money between the two jobs, and I wanted to put it to good use. I always had connections, and this one in particular always had large, high-quality batches he was willing to sell for cheap. I also knew four or five guys who would make these drives for awful cocaine and pay about $1,600 for an ounce, so I told them I could get an ounce of better stuff for $1,400 in town. I would tell them it wasn't me, so I needed the money up front, or that the guy was lending it to me so I needed the money in full when I brought it to them. If they believed that I was just doing them a favor, it reduced the risk of my not getting all the money.

The truth was that I was purchasing these bags for $900 out of pocket and making $500 on each sale.

Before too long I was rolling in money. I was even able to rent another house across the bridge from Burlington under someone else's name in order to stash the bulk of my cash and supply. My plan was to do this until Christmas, when I would have a hefty savings, and then call it quits.

Before I knew it, I was right back in it. "But this time is different," I would say. "I have plenty of cash to support me, I've got two jobs, and school. There is no way I can do more than I can spend." It wasn't the money that was the problem. It was my ego.

It probably only took a week. I told all the people I was selling to the truth. I was the actual connect and not just a middleman. I wanted to be "the boss" and have everyone looking to me for what they needed. Again, I felt I was needed, respected, feared, and loved. I could control how someone felt about me. It was the same as in high school, but on a much darker level. Without reserve, people began to ask for favors and price cuts and everything. The game had changed, and so had my mind.

I became dependent on pills again, and heroin came into the picture. It was cheaper, and it gave me the same effect as the pills. I couldn't get out of bed without getting a fix. During the day, the intervals between using had become shorter and shorter. I would even wake up in the middle of the night feeling dope-sick and have to get loaded.

OxyContin's price had risen to $80–$100 a pill since they were taking them off the market and replacing them with the OP pill. Every day, I went through seven to ten Oxy pills and an eight ball of cocaine. By blowing around $1,000 dollars a day, I burned through my savings. From there it didn't take long for my habit to outpace the money I was bringing in.

I needed to get out of town, and Thanksgiving break came at a perfect time.

I remember my dad telling me I looked slim when I arrived home, and I told him I had been running a lot. I had brought some pills home with me that should have lasted the few days I was there. However, my craving was so strong that I finished everything on the plane ride and the first night I arrived. I was barely functioning for Thanksgiving and slept the entire time my family and friends had Thanksgiving dinner right outside my room.

Starting to undergo withdrawal and feeling really irritable, I provoked my mother into an argument, and it escalated to a point where I can remember her standing at the top of the stairs, picking up a statue of a seahorse, which was almost bigger than she was, and heaving it at my head with all her might. I made her out to be the crazy one, when all she wanted was a peaceful Thanksgiving with her family. My father and my sister were in shock.

I left the next day and went back to Vermont. As soon as my feet hit Burlington, I got a fix and began to plan how I would survive until Christmas. I was vulnerable, but my pride would fuel me until the end. All I had to do was keep my parents believing that I was doing well in school and working, while making everybody else believe I was still this big drug boss who had what they needed.

Christmas could not come soon enough.

Alex

I am still working on forgiving my brother. Moving on and getting over it is one thing, but I have not been able to truly forgive him yet. I am still full of anger about the things he did to our family. I am still full of anger about the things he took away from our family.

Christmas of 2010 was quite possibly one of the worst days of my life. I stared at my parents' blank faces, speechless, across from my brother on the couch. He sat with a stack of gifts on his lap, limp arms at his side, and no emotion on his face. He was a corpse. A miserable, ungrateful, selfish corpse. He didn't care that we were all gathered around the Christmas tree having breakfast together. He didn't care about all the new ski gear my parents had bought him so he could have a "fun" winter. He didn't care that it was probably going to be the last year we were all together in the house we both grew up in. All he cared about was getting back to bed.

His face was completely caved in, and he was thinner than I had ever seen him, insisting that his new "sober" body wasn't as hungry as it was when he was using. I knew he was a liar and that rehab was the only option. But he promised he could do it on his own. The doubt that filled my mind made me so uneasy, but as his sister it was my duty to continue to support him. No matter how many times he let me down, I still continued to support him.

My brother spent 80 percent of the day in bed except to come down and eat Christmas dinner. Christmas that year was small, not like the past years when we would have thirty or more people over to feast. This year it was about family and close friends. One of the families that joined us had recently lost their mother and one of the boys was Mike's best friend, Jack. I can't even begin to imagine what they were going through, and I'm sure that all they wanted for the holidays was to be around happy, loving people. But everyone knew something was off, and I felt embarrassed the entire day. Not embarrassed for me but embarrassed for Mike. He was too messed up to feel it for himself. He was too messed up to pay attention to someone other than himself, not even his best friend who was silently in pain and needed him.

I couldn't wait to get back to California. Watching my parent's cry and scream was something I was not used to. A few years after I had moved to the West Coast, I started distancing myself from my brother and his addiction. I wanted to be far removed from it, so I guess I didn't realize how bad it actually was. But here I was again running back across the country because I didn't want to see him and his addiction tear my family apart.

Anita

When our friends arrived on Christmas Day, I barely looked at my son. I didn't want to see what I was afraid to look at. A usually festive holiday house was solemn as his friends and mine were so surprised by what they saw. My healthy, handsome, bright-eyed son was gone. He was pale and thin and almost unrecognizable. My friend Terri took me aside and said, "Look at your son. He needs help."

It was as if someone had stuck needles in my eyes. I knew my friend was right, and for the first time in his life, I didn't try to defend my son. I knew the situation was dire. A close friend of ours had passed away recently who was a loving mother to three beautiful boys. One of them was Mike's best friend, Jack. We had the boys over for Christmas day lunch, and I felt so sad that Mike was not even spending time with Jack. Mike was just not there for him, and it broke my heart. This is what I saw, and this is when I knew.

That was not my son.

Mike

I was driving back to the cape from Vermont for Christmas with my friend Lou. We took my car, but I was so loaded that I couldn't even keep my eyes open. I told Lou I was extremely tired and couldn't stop nodding off. We pulled over, and he drove the rest of the way. I slept the entire ride. We arrived on the cape later that night, and I can't remember if we did anything other than eat a lot of food. I hadn't been eating much other than sweet cinnamon rolls from the corner store by our house in Vermont.

The next day I was supposed to give Lou a ride home. But first, I had to get my morning fix. I ground up some of the OxyContin I had brought home with me and threw it on some tin foil to smoke in my bathroom. It smelled like nail polish remover. After I was done, I went downstairs to eat some food since I didn't feel so sick anymore.

My mother called my name from upstairs and called me into my room. "What's that smell?" she asked. I probably just responded with "What smell?" trying to pass it off. She knew something was up. She pulled out the foil and the pen. Lies spewed from my mouth about how "it's only an occasional thing."

When she persisted, I blamed it on Lou, who had never even touched the stuff. Somehow I managed to slip away to drive him home. I figured that it wasn't a big deal. I figured it happened, it was done, and that was that. I was wrong.

That whole day was a blur to me, but I assumed I tried to stay away from the house all day. That night I remember coming home to greet my dad on the couch, where I sat down to watch TV with him. He wanted to talk, and I didn't. He asked if I was smoking crack, and my response was, "*No,* it's just OxyContin," as if that was much better. I explained my delusion and false belief that I had just fallen back into it recently, but that this was my finish line and I would be starting fresh from that point on. I didn't want to talk anymore.

He wanted to talk, and I told him that now was not the right time. I was infuriating him, and he asked, "Well, when is the right time?" I began to get angry as well and yelled obscenities at him, telling him to just "shut the fuck up!" I pushed him to his limit. This man who would never hurt a fly was pushed over the edge by my disrespect and hideous selfishness.

My father got out of his seat and came toward me. I must have subconsciously known what I deserved was coming because I didn't even move. Next came a well-deserved punch to the face from my father. We wrestled around a little bit, and I finally broke free. I began to walk up the stairs, still believing I was in the right and yelling at my dad, saying he was the messed-up one. The rest is a blur.

The next morning I woke up to someone I recognized standing over me looking very angry. It was my buddy Bob. I had been avoiding him because I knew he had an idea of what was going on, and I didn't want to hear what I needed to. I was extremely cranky that morning and told him to leave me alone. A withdrawal was starting to kick in, and I didn't want to see anyone, not him, my parents, or my sister, who had just flown in all the way from California. I somehow got him to leave, but he said he would be back and that we would talk.

That whole day I was in and out of sleep, feeling sick and uncomfortable. Cold sweats kicked in. I remember fading in and out to different members of my family at my bedroom door, asking if I wanted to go out to dinner with them. I felt like they were taunting me. Half the time I'm sure I was hallucinating or dreaming it all. I had no energy, no life in me to get my ass out of bed to spend a Christmas Eve dinner with my family. At the time I didn't care. I just didn't want to feel like crap anymore. I didn't even have the energy to get a fix.

That night Bob came back. He told me to come with him for a ride. I got in his car.

We drove down the dirt back road to my house. He stopped, looked at me, and gave me a nice whack to the face to wake me up. Well deserved. He pulled the car around and pulled up facing my house. With his care for me, he tried to open my eyes and help me understand all the harm I was causing. He said things like, "Look at what you're doing to your family. You wouldn't have this nice cushion to come home to and be a selfish prick if it weren't for your parents. They love and care for you so much, and you are just throwing it in their face. You don't give a crap about anyone but yourself anymore."

It hurt. He was right.

We went to the Fox Hole over in Osterville so I could see some friends and see how many people actually cared about me. We spent a little time there, and later he dropped me back off at my house.

Christmas morning, I woke up sore and exhausted. I was a little more coherent but still felt like a decrepit old man. Christmas is supposed to be a fun and happy time, yet I had not a shred of joy in my heart. How could I? I had nothing to offer. I had caused all this pain and agony, yet my parents still had smiles on their faces as they handed me gifts. "I don't deserve this," I thought to myself. I could no longer even be grateful for what was right in front of me. I didn't want to feel like that anymore.

This time I thought for sure was the end and that I would somehow magically go back to school and sober up. I believed it with all my heart. If you had hooked me up to a lie detector test, I would have been telling the truth. But I wasn't worried too much about school yet. I still had a couple of weeks of Christmas break where I could get loaded before I went back to school.

After all, Phish was about to be playing at Madison Square Garden in New York City for a few nights and for New Year's Eve.

After a few nights of Phish at Madison Square Garden and the new year upon us, I went back to

Burlington with my new resolution to focus on school and forget about everything else.

Oh, and I was going to be "sober from pills and heroin."

Anita

Mike left in January to go back to Vermont. I wasn't prepared for how I would feel when we got back to New York City. It all hit me so hard. Most days I couldn't get out of bed. I was so petrified and freaked out about my heart, the bills, my son, and what was going to happen to my family. I literally shut down and, on certain days, wished that I would die.

I was missing my daughter terribly. She had gone back to Los Angeles and was starting a new job. She had been working hard and had a new apartment while making her way in life. It was so upsetting to me that I couldn't help her out more that I would wake up in the middle of the night from horrible nightmares. That Christmas had been so special for her to fly home and be with us all for the last Christmas in our family home, and her brother had ruined her entire trip.

I realized how we had been paying so much attention to Mike that we were neglecting our daughter. For so long it seemed that every time she would call to talk about her life and typical twenty-something stuff, I would always throw in, "Have you talked to your brother today? How does he sound to you?" That's all I could focus on.

I was addicted to my son's addiction.

I never realized how much anger she had brewing inside of her until the family therapy at Caron. She didn't deserve it and had had more than enough of it all. I felt like she was the lucky one that got to board that plane and get away from it all and never thought about how she needed her parents more than ever. I felt like I was the child and needed my daughter in a whole new way. Overnight she had become my best friend and confidant, just as my own mother and I had been.

Between hiding things from my husband and Alex being so far away, I felt very alone and scared. My anger for my son was so unbearable at that point that I couldn't wait for something to happen to make him realize things had to change. I was so tired of being handcuffed to the heavy dread that I actually felt paralyzed with fear on certain days. All the while, our birthdays and anniversaries were slipping by as if they were just another day on the calendar. Time was passing by quickly, and that made me even more frightened. The only thing that frightened me more was that I had no idea what to do to help my son. I felt completely useless, which was something I was not used to.

I knew from friends that had been through this with their own children that nothing would work until Mike wanted the help. I had to wait and pray no one would die before that happened.

Mike

I had no money to buy coke and sell to people, or even to get any dope to get loaded, so it shouldn't have been that hard to make a fresh start, only I wasn't going to give up that easily. I was a selfish, dishonest, manipulative drug addict. Had having no money ever stopped me before? Had a firm resolution to stop using drugs and alcohol ever kept me sober before? *No!* And it wasn't about to this time. So what mischievous schemes could I come up with this time?

"OK, what can I sell?" My MacBook Pro, a few iPods, and a few other trinkets. Perfect! I was then able to find a quick fix, and with OxyContin so expensive, I had to resort to some low-quality heroin. However, it gave me what I was looking for: the will and strength to bring down whoever I could while I was on this spiral of self-sabotage. So I stole, and I stole a lot from roommates and friends alike, and continued to sell their computers and instruments. "They should have seen it coming," I'd say. "I'll hopefully be dead in a week anyway," I'd sadly tell myself. I was trying to make this last run the end of the road for me. I saw no other choice.

I began to go to the homeless shelter and soup kitchen around the corner from my house. This was not to help out but to seek refuge and stay out of the way of anyone I may have robbed. "Clever," I thought to myself, "no one would think that I could have fallen low enough to have to stay at a homeless shelter. They'll never find me here." This pattern continued for the first two weeks. By the end of that second week, a series of bad decisions and events would soon seal my fate.

Panic was right by my side, but still an awkward and prideful cockiness followed. I had a friend pick me up by an old buddy's house while I hid in the snow, thinking that every headlight that went by was someone out to get me. Then my friend suddenly pulled up. First stop was finding a ticket to Hawaii, where, if I survived all this, I would go to start yet another new life. However, until the departure in two days, I would find myself at a broken-down Motel 6, where I would seek protection and refresh my drug supply during my last day in town.

Then the text from my mother came. I had written her saying, "No one can help me."

CHAPTER 6

ERASING THE PAST

Anita

Now, with Mike safely tucked away at the Caron Treatment Center in Pennsylvania, we, my son included, knew it was the only kind of help that would save his life. Our insurance company, however, had other ideas.

With Mike in treatment, my new routine was waiting for my husband to leave so I could start responding to the mysterious texts I kept receiving about the money Mike owed. I didn't even stop to question how these people suddenly had my cell number. I was calling his landlord to try and get him out of his lease and contacting the friends he'd stolen from. I was going up to Vermont to deal with people I'd never met, people I couldn't picture my son knowing, to try and set things right. It was a spy's routine, one I couldn't share with my daughter or my husband, and certainly not one I could share with Mike. I just wanted to make it all go away.

Unable to include anyone in my family, I asked George, a producer friend, to drive me up to Burlington. Instead of going up for my son's graduation, I was going to clean up the mess he had made of his life. It was a trip I couldn't imagine making three years earlier when we dropped him off for his freshman year.

As George drove onto the on-ramp of the highway to hell, we ended up in the middle of a blizzard. I closed my eyes and reflected on everything that was happening in my life. I remembered that my friend Brooke had once said to me, "Welcome to the Fuck-You Fifties." She couldn't have been more right. That's exactly where I was. Brooke was the one I would talk to every morning at six a.m. about life and she would give me most of my material for the blog posts I would write. Another friend I was grateful for. But at this particular moment I wasn't grateful for anything. The only thing I was feeling was bitterness.

The dog show was the only thing I had to look forward to, and I jumped when I heard my cell ringing. It was the show runner. He said, "We are good to go! Let's sign the last contract and celebrate when you get back."

"Just one little thing though," he said.

I didn't like the sound of it.

"The network is fine with everything, but they want the show to be *edgier*. We want dogs fighting, dog walkers fighting and dog action."

I was crushed.

It was the exact opposite of the vision we all had for the show. Mailer, our investor and I refused to do it. Since we had only pitched to one network, and it had been picked up so fast, we reasoned that we would start over and pitch it to other networks. We wouldn't compromise. We would only show the loving, caring side of the dog walkers.

So now, while driving through a whiteout blizzard on the way to clean up my son's drug den in Vermont, my contract was cancelled. If I hadn't felt a big black cloud following me before, I certainly did now. The evil eye was a definite possibility. I felt cursed. I couldn't think of any other explanation for all the bad things that were happening.

I needed to get to Vermont, pay everyone my son owed money to, grab his stuff, clean his room out, and get back to New York City to get out and pitch the show again. As the snow was freezing on our wipers, I watched the other cars skidding by side to side as if in slow motion.

My hand was trembling as I called my husband and gave him the bad news. Had I made the right decision? Should I have done it for the money?

Michael agreed with me and thought the same thing I did.

"If you sold it that quickly, then we will sell it again. The right way," he said. I didn't respond. It should have been a normal, easy conversation, the way everything used to be between Michael and me. Now, in the silence, I knew neither one of us was thinking about anything other than our son. Our lives had become consumed by addiction. It filled up every room and pushed everything else out.

George and I finally arrived in Burlington at Mike's house and tried to focus. Upon entering, I climbed up the stairs to my son's room. One by one. Slower than I'd done anything in my life. When I finally opened the door, my legs wouldn't move. They didn't want to take me in. They wanted to run the other way. I stood there staring at what used to be my son's room.

It looked like it belonged in a horror movie.

I could taste the vomit climbing in my throat as my head started to spin. My friend George came running up the stairs and almost crashed into me as I dove into the mildewed, filthy bathroom, vomiting over and over again. The most "courageous mother moments" of my life did not come close to what I had in front of me in that dark, dreary hallway of this house in Vermont.

"Thank God my husband is not here to see this," I thought to myself. After all the hell my son has put my family through, why am I protecting him by not telling my husband and daughter all that I know or all that I've seen?

Am I protecting him or them?

Mothers protect everyone but themselves. I know I've said it many times in my life and have heard other women say it as well. When do we get one little minute of our lives that does not involve worrying about someone else?

I was somewhere in my head that I didn't have a name for, somewhere I needed to dwell to avoid the harshness of my son's former reality.

Looking around Mike's room and the task ahead of me, I realized that I wasn't sad anymore. I wasn't confused or worried. I felt extreme hatred for my son. Hatred like I had never felt before. I didn't even judge myself for feeling that way. I hated him and didn't care.

I only knew one thing at that moment. I wanted to get out of that house as quickly as possible and find a hypnotist that could erase the entire experience from my memory.

My poor friend George was quietly going through this room of garbage. There was nothing that I recognized that would make me believe this was my son's room. Where were his family photos, photos of friends, the lamps, the mirrors, his clothes, his new sheets?

My anger boiled over thinking that the university took our check for $40,000 without informing us that our son was not showing up for classes. I silently raged, thinking about our child talking to a therapist for $250 an hour while he was stoned, blaming everything on his parents. I raged over the insurance company not paying for rehab because they said Mike didn't need to be there. It all made me sick.

I felt like a victim. A victim who wanted to lash out.

Mike was in Pennsylvania working through his addiction at rehab. My daughter was in Los Angeles working at her brand-new job. My husband was in New York City, working and going about his daily routine, while I, the mother, was standing in a pile of filthy drug paraphernalia in this shithole room in Burlington, Vermont.

I started throwing everything and anything into garbage bags.

His old life had been packed in boxes and shoved into the back of a dark, mold-filled basement: high school yearbooks, lacrosse awards, family photos, schoolbooks, and his clothes. We carried the brand-new mattress—which was ripped open—out to the garbage along with the broken desk and broken chair and bag after bag of plastic baggies, pen cartridges, and foil.

I called the landlord and told him Mike wouldn't be coming back and that the roommates were going to find a replacement. He was such a kind man, and I told him the truth about what had happened. I can remember getting a beautiful card from him and his wife with a blessing in it that let me know they had dealt with struggles in their own family. They understood.

I wrote checks to his roommates for stolen laptops and missing money. I met with the creeps that Mike owed money to and paid them off. I went to the hospital and got his medical records. I got on my hands and knees and bleached his disgusting room. Garbage bag after garbage bag of crap was lined up for the sanitation department to haul out of our lives forever.

I was so grateful to have George on this road trip with me. He never said the wrong thing. Having him by my side that day kept me together. Being a producer, he knew what a difficult decision it was for me to back out of the dog show deal, but he talked me down off the cliff on our ride back home by telling me that I made the right decision. I was thinking that I'd get home and go out and pitch it and sell it again.

I was thinking life would start moving forward again and that the past was lined up on the street in garbage bags.

CHAPTER 7

THE COST OF GUILT

Once I returned to New York, there was an eerie sense of calm.

Mike was making great progress, and the counselors were calling to keep us updated. They said that Mike needed to be there, and we were all thankful he was getting the treatment he needed. What I was not thankful for was the insurance company insisting that he didn't need to be there and that they would not reimburse us.

I sent in mounds and mounds of paperwork with letter after letter from doctors saying that it was a medical necessity for Mike to be at Caron. We sent in proof that he had done the outpatient program leading up to this, which was a requirement. Perhaps I should have videotaped Mike on Christmas Day and taken photos of his room. There would have been no doubt then.

Every day I would call doctors, get letters, call hospitals, get records, call therapists, get more verification letters, and send everything to our insurance company. We did three levels of appeals that weighed about ten pounds, stating that he needed to be at Caron. All we received was $3,000 for his first three days in treatment.

We weren't reimbursed for any of the outpatient treatment leading up to inpatient or for any of the doctors in between. They didn't even reimburse us for the asshole therapist who told my husband and me that we put too much pressure on Mike and to give him some space. Another idiot. Another doctor putting the blame on parents to the tune of $250 per hour.

I went to see my own doctor because I was so afraid of how I felt. I had been having such horrific mood swings that I was scared. I was moving toward menopause I was told. Oh, what joy! More good news for Mom! There would be no taking hormones for me because of my mother's breast cancer and I would just have to work through it. Perfect. Just add it to the list.

My anger was so out of control, and I was so sick of the endless mounds of paperwork and phone calls that I couldn't get a grip. I had no idea where the money was going to come from, and I had such tremendous guilt about turning down the network offer for the dog show. I was sinking deeper and deeper into a dark, scary hole of guilt.

Looking back, I realize that even my son, as messed up as he was, was constantly trying to help his friends that were in the same boat he was in. I didn't even stop to think back then that he was in the same boat as well because I watched the things he did for his troubled friends. The children of my friends.

My friends who were so busy talking about Mike that they were ignoring what was going on with their own children. I now realize that I was doing the same thing. The only difference is that I wasn't talking about their kids.

That is an evil trait for a mother to have. Thankfully, my memory is long.

We were gearing up for our first visit to Caron to see Mike after his first two weeks of treatment.

We had to write him cost letters beforehand, and I was looking forward to that. My poor daughter had to leave her brand-new job in Los Angeles to fly home for the family therapy. She wanted to be there for her brother and also for herself.

Mike

I started receiving cost letters from my family. I would hear of how I had harmed them. In the beginning, I was still an emotionless shell, and I didn't feel much about them other than using humor to bat away what I was really feeling. It took me some time, but after the primary feeling of anger during this time of treatment went away, I started to feel the guilt and shame over everything that I had done. I knew that if I was to move forward, I had to clean up the wreckage of my past and make things right with those I harmed.

The cost letter that opened my eyes the most was from my sister. She finally let me know how she felt. She felt lonely out in California since all the family's attention was on me. She reminded me of my selfishness. She explained how many times she wanted to separate herself from our family because of my antics. I began to feel very guilty, and I was ashamed of myself. Alex and I had always had a special relationship. We actually got along more than we fought. It pained me to realize that I had pushed her so far away, and I was fearful that we would never be close again. I was envious of her and how well she had her shit together and wondered why I couldn't do that. I felt like a failure compared to her.

Alex always persevered and never gave up on anything. I would constantly pick things up and put them down before ever completing anything. If I made a mistake, I would avoid that situation. If my sister made a mistake, she held her head high and worked through it. I wished I could be like her. My shame and insecurity had such a hold on me that I couldn't do what she could do.

I did what made me feel right instead. Drugs.

Alex always seemed to know what she wanted to do and was beginning to do it all. I never had any self-direction or goals as to where I wanted to be, and even if I did, I was so afraid of failing that I would give up and stop trying. The only thing I was good at doing was drugs.

The first day I was allowed to have visitors at Caron, Aunt Seva and Uncle Al came to visit me. I was so happy to see them, but at the same time I had trouble holding back the tears of my guilt and shame. They were such good people and lived so simply. It seemed like life had come easily to them, and instead of doing, they just were. I wished so badly I could be just like them. I was ashamed of myself and had done so many bad things, and yet these two humble souls continued to love me just the same. In these types of moments, shame could drive me in one of two ways. I could either drown it with drugs or find a new, healthy solution.

Anita
This is the first letter Michael and I received from Mike after his first weekend at Caron.

Ma and Pa Dukes,

It's Monday. Made it through the weekend.
First off I want to apologize for never getting
clearer handwriting. You can yell at me in the
next letter you write to me...thank God I won't
get it for about a week.

Anyway, so far so good. Most of the other
young "gentlemen" here are characters. They
want to be here, yet they say they would
rather be in prison. "I hate the fact that I'm in

a rehab." I try to tell them "it's a pretty nice rehab!" Ha! I just am actually glad to be here and that I'm under great care. Seeing so many kids with their negativity makes me realize more and more that I'll be all right. It's just something I'll have to work at my entire life, and I am fine with it.

We went to chapel yesterday morning. Like nothing I've ever been to. Kind of like an AA meeting/talent show/church but without specific religions. You guys will see it when you come for the parents' family week, which by the way I hear is nothing to look forward to. But if it helps us grow and understand our relationships to a greater extent, I'm all for it.

Most of the patients can't understand why and how I'm so optimistic about this. I tell them that if I wasn't, I may be back out there just throwing my life away. I am here because of a "choice." A choice based off a reason. A reason because there is something I'd like to change in my life and I have not been happy with any of my choices. However, I am happier than ever that I made this choice.

I love you guys more than anything in the world. The only thing I am happier about is that you guys are willing to take this ride with me. Thank you so much, and I hope to hear from you soon. I love you, and tell Alex and Skilo I love them too.

Love,
Mikey

I didn't believe anything he said. To me he was a manipulative liar, and I was done being an idiot.

About two weeks later, I noticed a change in his writing.

Mom,

I cannot describe the sadness I feel when I sit and think about the hurt I've put you through. All you've ever wanted was the best for me, and I feel as though I've spat in your face with all the lies and manipulation. I am being taught to recognize these faults and put them in the past and to move on to work in a more positive manner. We cannot change the past, but we can change our behavior. In the situation with you, it burns me up when I think about you. You are my mother, and yet I continue to neglect that fact and embarrass you beyond reason, yet you still stand by me with unconditional love.

I cannot believe how blind I was to the stubbornness and selfishness that I brought. My eyes are open to this fact now, and it crushes me to realize the pain and suffering that I put into your heart. I hate to blame any of this on my addiction; however, I can only blame it on myself.

For years I have used drugs to fill a void in my heart I that I could not explain, and yet it has only created a bigger one. This grew into an uncontrollable habit and well past abuse. I am not Mike when I am using…I am my own and your worst enemy.

I am not going to get into all the ways I hurt you, for that will all come in time, and it will take me days to write. However I want to let you know that you were always right. I wish I had never started using. I wish I had never hurt you dad and Alex the way I have. I cannot change this, and the only way now is to recognize these faults and to rise above and move forward.

I hate the person I've become, and I look forward to the progress that is to come. I'm not saying I will ever be perfect, but I promise I will do my very best to reach into the darkest pits my heart and bring forth your son.

Addiction is a disease, and I see now I have no control over my abuse of pills. I have believed for so long for them to be my survival, but in reality they were my downfall—my ever-awaiting death—destroying me and everyone that cares for me. I just want to get better because *I can't do this anymore!* All I want is to have my family back and to sit beside you, pa dukes, and my big sis. I cannot pretend to have the ability to do this on my own anymore. Nevertheless, I will put my strongest effort into working the steps and to walk with you as not only a human being but as your son.

I'm sorry, Mom; I truly am. I miss you so much, and I miss myself. I thank you for sticking by me to fight this issue through to the end. This is only the beginning of my thanks and my apology, for I do not deserve your forgiveness. I hope that one day it is truly able to be earned.

So for now, keep that strength that you have never lost, and I shall build mine. Please give Dad and Skilo a big hug and kiss from me. You guys are my family. I feel ready without fear and doubt to overcome this enemy. Stay strong.

Your son,
Mikey

A few days later, a letter for Michael came.

Pa Dukes,

Seventh day at Caron and feeling pretty good physically, mentally...pretty stable. Emotionally, a little distraught at the moment...thinking about you a lot.

I just got out of a medium-sized group meeting where I let go pretty seriously. I opened up big time about Christmas Eve. Gave the whole breakdown, and I couldn't help but keep feeling increasingly guilty and resentful for what I had done and to where I had pushed you. You always taught me to bite my tongue in any controversy, especially with Mom. You always taught me to hold back my anger and to just say sorry. You truly are the kindest and most openhearted man I know.

To hear the recap of Christmas play out from my mouth...I couldn't believe my words describing your anger and my selfishness. To see you break to a level of anger that high showed me how much I had sunk to a new low that I can never take back. I can't believe I had not seen the severity of my addiction at that time, and I cannot take back what has been done. I have a problem with pills, and it is jeopardizing me, you, and our entire livelihood and I am sick of it.

I cannot do this on my own, and I have realized that more and more. You say it is will power; however, addiction is something much greater. I cannot conquer my usage and demons alone, but I know that I stand a fighting chance with the help of my friends, family, and the people at Caron. Together I hope we can conquer this and move on to a greater good and means.

I love you with all my heart, and I will use all of my willpower to stay on the right track.

Love,
Your son,
Little Mike

CHAPTER 8

THE SHATTERED SIBLING

Anita

Writing a cost letter is not what it sounds like. It is not about how much the addiction cost you in monetary value but rather what it has cost you emotionally, spiritually, physically, and mentally. As a family and as an individual, you have lost things along the way. I reached out to Mike's best friends and certain family members asking them to write him as well. I wanted him to receive letters from people whom I knew were going to tell the truth about the destruction he had caused. It was not the time for flowers, poems, or fiction. I remember sitting at my laptop and looking at our family dog, who had loved Mike so much but was more afraid of him as his using progressed. Yes, I wrote Mike the cost letter below, but since I was menopausal, I thought

I had a right to do it. I never imagined how huge the impact would be for anyone that reads it.

Dear Mikey,

Maybe this is the first time someone in treatment has received a letter from a family member like me. I feel that I am a part of this family and that your behavior has affected me as much as anyone else. I came to live with you six years ago, which is when I think your drug problems were beginning.

I can remember living in Georgia, watching my eleven brothers and sisters being adopted, and I was left all alone because I was the smallest and the weakest. No one wanted me, and I was scared. One day I overheard a conversation on the phone about a family's dog passing away and that the one left behind was very sad and lonely. They were looking for someone to keep him company. I had no idea where Cape Cod was, and I was petrified to go on an airplane by myself. I only knew that I was on my way to live with a special family and a boy named Mikey.

It was not long after I arrived that your dog Brewster passed away. I knew that the family

dogs were closest to you. Winston would sit
every day with his nose through the fence
waiting for you to come home from school. You
would take them for rides and play together
in the backyard for hours on end. I also know
that you were the one that would help them get
up on Mom and Dad's bed at night when they
were old and in pain and couldn't get up by
themselves anymore.

When Brewster passed away, you and I became
best friends. I would wait for you to come home
from school and whistle our private sound
so that I could follow you. We would swim
together and play lacrosse together, and I would
snuggle up with you to watch movies. I would
always wedge myself between you and your
girlfriends on the couch because I knew I really
was your "only" girl.

I was the luckiest dog on the planet.

One day that all changed. You went away to
college, and when you would come home, it
wasn't fun anymore. You ignored all of us and
were mean and angry all the time. There was
no more playing in the backyard. There was
just a lot of fighting and yelling. Now instead
of laying with you on the couch, I would

instead lay with Mom so she could squeeze
and hold me tight. She would cry so hard that
my head would be soaked from her tears. This
happened all the time. You would just create a
big mess and leave. I couldn't wait for you to go
away.

There was a time when I would get so excited
when Mom or Dad would say, "Mikey's
coming home!" But now when I hear you are
coming home, I start to shake. I know you
see me hiding in the corner or outside behind
the bushes. I know you see me with my tail
between my legs as I tremble. Your yelling
and screaming at Mom and Dad has made me
want to jump out and bite you many times.
The only reason I didn't was because I may
have been sent away, and Mom would not have
me to cry on anymore. I am supposed to have
unconditional love, but instead I hated you.

I hear Mom, Dad, and Alex talking now about
how you are away somewhere because you want
to get better. I hope you do because I miss the
Mikey I first came to live with. I am getting
older now, and soon I won't be able to run
around in the backyard or swim anymore. I too
am going to need help getting up on Mom and
Dad's bed at night. So please get better and

come home before it's too late. I'm waiting for you.

Love,
Your best friend, Skilo

The counselors receive the letters and read them first, and then the boys take turns reading each other's aloud in group. I can only imagine Mike's humiliation when someone stood up and read his letter from the family dog. I was hanging tight in the angry corner of my mind, and writing the letters gave me some relief. The first one I wrote was when he first got to Caron, and it was a letter of encouragement. The second one I wrote was not so nice.

Alex

My brother was at a rehab in Pennsylvania. I couldn't believe this was happening to our family. But even more so, I couldn't believe this was happening to our parents. All my parents ever gave us was unconditional love. They never said no, they never argued, and they never judged.

They always trusted us, loved us, and gave us everything we needed and so much more. Two selfless people who worked hard their entire lives to build a family were watching it crumble before their very eyes. And there was nothing anyone could do about it except Mike.

I had just started a new job, and within a week I was already being told I had to fly home for three days to attend family week at Mike's rehab. I could not believe that I was dropping everything and risking my new job for him, but he needed me more than ever. I told myself and my family that this was his last chance. I needed to look Mike in the eyes and make sure he really understood that.

Before I went to family weekend, I had to send Mike a cost letter. I didn't know what that meant exactly, but I took it as "What has addiction cost you?" I wrote him just that.

Mikey,

I sat down to write this letter, and I am
immediately in tears. There have been so many
things I've wanted to say to you for the past
five or six years that I've never said because
I've been too scared of what could happen if
I actually said them. I've realized now that
maybe I should have told you all of this,
because maybe you wouldn't be in this current
spot. But I can't look back and try to change
the past and act like anything I did or said may
have been able to help you.

You are where you are now because of the
choices and decisions *you* have made. There is

no one else to blame. And I am so happy that you've chosen to finally admit that you have a problem and that you are strong enough to fix it.

I've talked this letter out to myself a thousand times, but now that I am actually finally sitting down to tell it to you, it feels different. I want you to know before reading what you are about to read that no matter where you have put yourself in life, and no matter how angry I am with you, I still love you madly and have complete confidence that you can beat this. You are my little brother. No matter how you write the story of your life, that will never change.

Remember the day that your lacrosse team beat Falmouth and you scored the winning goal? I jumped so high that day cheering for you I thought I was flying. I've never been so proud of anyone in my life. I've never felt such joy and excitement for another person. I told you that day that you were my hero. Moments later, when I got home, I found a letter in the mail telling me I was accepted to Emerson. My dream. You then called me and told me I was your hero. I can't remember the last time I felt like that with you...that might have been the last time I felt like I had a brother.

Everything was always so easy for you when we were growing up. You were smart and didn't try, great at sports, had a million friends, and were just cool. I sort of felt like in some ways that you were my older brother. I didn't really ever feel like I had to take care of you. But a big part of that was because in high school, I just felt like I didn't *want* to take care of you. You were, for lack of a better word, a nightmare. I knew on your second day of fifth grade when you refused to wear your St. Francis uniform that you were going to be difficult. I can't even remember how many fights and arguments you had with Mom and Dad. Or how short and cold you were to everyone in this family. Or how many times you lied or screamed or cared about every other person in the world besides the people in your family. I can't remember the last time you participated in being a member of our family. And I'm sick of it. I always wanted more siblings because I felt like I had no relationship with you. I always tried and wanted to be a part of your life, but you never really wanted to have me around. Until I left for college and you realized you were alone in the house. I'd come home and you'd finally want to hang out with me, but I didn't want to hang out with you. Funny how something I waited for my entire life was no longer something I even thought about anymore. I wanted to hang out with the people who actually did want to be around me in high school and middle school. I didn't want to go out to bars with you and your friends. I felt like you would just want to hang out so you could say you saw me while I was home. Like it was a good deed. Well, I have *one* brother. And that actually means something to me. Having a family that cares about each other and participates in each other's lives is the most important thing to me. Obviously, no family is perfect, and ours could have been close to it, but you really shattered that quickly.

I'm sorry if you feel this is harsh, but I think you need to truly start to understand the damage that has been caused, that you have been so blind to see. I listened to you talk about how you wanted to help your friends that were going through the same things you are on the way up to Boston, and the whole time I thought to myself, "What are you talking about? You are more messed up than all of them, and you don't even see it." The difference is, you are the luckiest shit in the world, because you have three people who are willing to take all the crap that you've thrown on us, and still stand up for you and want to help you at the end of the day.

Do you have any idea how lucky you are, that
you have two of the most amazing people on this
planet for your parents? Two people who have
given up almost everything they have worked
their whole lives for to help you? And you for
so long thought that all the nagging and all
the questions were because they were annoying.
Without them, you would be dead. I take no
credit for any help you've received, because I live
in California and have shut this out of my life
because I refused to allow your damage to be a
part of my life. But Mom and Dad couldn't do
that. You are their only son. Mom and Dad are
selfless.

Don't you think I want my family to come
visit me in California? Don't you think that
I want them to come see everything that I've
been working so hard to build on my own?
And finally be proud of me or pay some type of
attention to me without you ruining it?

Christmas Eve and Day, I tried to have so much
fun with our parents. We spent all Christmas
Eve together just enjoying each other's company.
But every time I looked at Mom and Dad, I
saw behind their eyes that their minds were
elsewhere. They were on you, since you refused
to get out of bed because you had been so

messed up for the days before you came home.
I flew three thousand miles to see my family,
and instead I sat in bed with Mom and Dad on
Christmas Day while they both cried to me.

My whole trip home consisted of me listening
to numerous conversations with what they
can do for you. I couldn't even talk about
anything that I've been doing, because no one
was interested. They were too concerned with
your well-being. I finally said out loud, "Who
the hell cares about this kid? He's ruined
everything, and you still continue to help
him?"

I'm extremely angry with you and what you have
done. I'm at a place in my life where I too am
struggling with making it through each day, but
for different reasons. You probably think that
everything gets handed to me, and that I don't
care about anything else, just my work. You've
told me numerous amounts of times to just
always stay the same and never let LA change
me. I am so lucky because of the opportunities
that have been given to me my whole life. Every
job I ever had, every person I ever met, has been
a part of my journey and I never took anything
for granted. I was driven, and I worked hard.
And now I feel like I'm being punished.

Because I have to take time out of my focus and
once again, my mind is now on you. My mind
is on you, worrying about you every single day.
And I can't call Mom and Dad and ask for
money to help me pay my rent, because they
have to clean up some mess you've made. You
never kept a job; you never finished anything
you started. You allowed pills to take over your
mind, body, and soul.

Where is that boy that scored that winning goal?

You gave up a huge part of your soul when you
realized lacrosse would no longer be easy for
you because of your injuries. The minute things
got hard, you bailed and turned to something
you thought would make you stronger and
forget about the pain. I have to tell you
something—there are other things in life that
you can be good at. There are other things in
life to love.

My whole life I wanted to be an actress. I
craved it; I loved it. I wanted to be famous
and for everyone to know my name. Not a
day passes where I don't have a moment that
I think about what my life would be like if I
hadn't given up that dream. I get teary eyed
for a second, pause and think about myself on

a stage somewhere, smile, and then come back to reality. I blame no one for that dream not coming true but myself.

But I didn't turn to things that could harm me. I found something else I'm good at and something else I love. I never lost my passion. My fire. My desire to succeed. You did. When that dream died, you died. You tried to mask it with your new major and going off to college, but I could always tell there was a part of you missing. I thought maybe it was depression that overcame you. But I now know that it was just drugs.

I realized how severe the problem was when I flew home to see Mom after her heart attack. You spent twenty minutes screaming at her on the back porch in front of me, Dad, and Mom's friends. It was the first time I felt embarrassed because of you. I thought, Who is this monster? Who is this selfish little shit that would give Mom any amount of stress after she'd just had a heart attack? That's when I realized...this had to stop.

Your bad attitude toward life, your excuses, your lies, your selfishness, your disease, ends today. You are *better* than all that. You have been given every tool needed to get better, so what are you going to do with them?

Show me a guy that deserves another chance. Because I'm willing to give it. But this is it. This is your last chance. I can't do this anymore. I refuse to watch Mom and Dad for the rest of their lives be worried about your health. I refuse to let your disease control my life. If this doesn't get better, I can't be a part of this any longer.

Everyone in this family deserves an apology. I feel like you've apologized to a lot of people, but never to me. I've never judged you or thought you were less of a person. I always tried to play devil's advocate, though I would normally side with our parents. But you were most of the time in the wrong, and I hope you see that now.

This will be the hardest thing you will ever have to do in your life. You are forever changed. Every single day for the rest of your life is going to be a struggle, but you need to be strong every single day to make it through. And know that *this* is *not* you. Find yourself. Get up every morning with intention. And take it one day at a time. There is no other way. Some days will be good, some will be great. Others will be

dark, and hard. But you cannot give up. You
need to fight away those bad days. Find things
that make you happy. Do things that give you
self-worth. And if you can do that, then you
will have a sister with you every step of the
way. You will have a cheerleader. I will give you
extra strength on the days you are feeling low, I
will send you love when you need it most, and
I will carry you when can't pick yourself up.
But only if you show me that you want to live a
good, full life.

I want my brother back. I want to be able to
sit at dinner with you, Mom and Dad and to
talk about anything but your disease. I want
to know about the exciting things that you are
doing. I want to be happy for you. I want to be
happy *with* you.

So go into this with an open mind and an
open heart. Be willing to allow people to help
you, allow people to care about you. Pray for
strength, and you'll get it. Fight to be better,
and you'll be there. And most importantly,
show us that you are the kid we all know you
are. Be my hero again.

Love you madly,
Cookie

Anita

Dear Mikey,

This is the hardest letter I have ever had to write in my life so far, but I know that it has to be done to help you get to where you need to be. Thinking of you and what you have to get through over these next few weeks is where I get my strength from, because what you have set out to accomplish makes my statement sound ridiculous.

I feel that as a mother I have failed to keep you safe and from harm's way. I know that whenever you asked me for help, I was always there to provide it for you. I was always so proud of you for asking for help when you felt you couldn't handle things on your own. But I also question myself, wondering if I missed or ignored some signs along the way to let me know that you needed more help than I thought.

You were always my shining star, even as a little boy. You were always smarter, cuter, and sweeter than any of your friends. You never had to struggle for good grades, friends, girlfriends, or anything for that matter. You always had the whole package from a very young age. I know

that during your childhood you and your sister
had a lot to deal with when I moved you up
to the cape. When my mother died, I couldn't
deal with my own depression and had to make
a decision for my well-being and that was to be
taken care of by my aunts, uncles, and cousins,
who, as you see, still all take care of each other.
If I didn't get the help I needed, I would not
be able to take care of you and Alex. I had
taken care of your grandmother for over eight
years and watched her physically disappear
from me day by day from cancer. This is how
I understand now about drugs being an illness
because I see the same thing happening with
you. The difference is that you can make it
stop. My mother couldn't.

I was so blessed to have the most amazing
relationship with my mother, as you and I have
the same, and I was so angry that I lost her that
I shut out everyone. I even shut out your father.
He put up with a lot from me for a long time, and
it was only until I realized with the help of my
family that I needed to seek counseling or I would
lose all that I loved the most in life if I did not get
professional help. I too, like you, felt I could do it
on my own. I too, like you, help everyone else with
their problems but couldn't help myself. Your true
friends will emerge in your new life and remain

there forever, but the ones that can't believe you are helping yourself now and not taking care of them will disappear from your life. Believe it or not, that will be a blessing.

I was so amazed at how quickly after putting myself into someone else's hands, so many truths about myself came to the surface for me. I had been avoiding my feelings and thoughts by staying very busy building a restaurant and working, just as you hide behind the pills, afraid to confront your truths about yourself. I can still remember the day I knew that I wanted out of the place I was in life. My best friend at the time, made me call your father and tell him I loved him and missed him. I did, but was afraid to tell him. Your father, who is by far the greatest man on earth, had never given up on me and was at our front door that day. This was the first day of the rest of my life.

You and I are fortunate to be allowed, by the grace of God and the love of our family, a new beginning because of the faith they have in us. Now as I sit back and watch so many of my dearest friends moving toward uncertain futures, I know how thankful I am and proud of myself for seeking the help I needed in order to save my marriage and my family, just as you are doing now. I love you, your sister, and your father more than anything in the world, and I thank God every day for you all.

I feel that when you were unable to play lacrosse due to the injuries, you started feeling very low. You did not stop playing because you were not good at it; you were an outstanding player but unfortunately had injury after injury. Instead of working out with trainers to strengthen supporting muscles and playing club, you seemed to just give up and spiral into someone I did not recognize. Your entire appearance changed. Your friends seemed to change as well. Unfortunately you were far away with a promising future that you were flushing down the toilet every chance you got. We reached out to your school therapist for your well-being and thought things were changing when you started counseling with her. All along I thought this was depression. It all was happening as your father's company closed and we were struggling to pay our bills. Our only commitment was to keep you and your sister in school for your future well-being. I was borrowing money to send to you because you said you could not find a job. We were so stressed out that I ended up having a heart attack last summer. I almost died. This

was a turning point in my relationship with
you. Who was this young man that instead of
helping me kept asking for more and more?

We found jobs for you that you couldn't keep.
Friends would go out on a limb for you and
hire you, but you kept letting them down. And
all along I would make excuse after excuse
for you because of my embarrassment and
disappointment. I was always waiting for the
son we missed so much to pop up somewhere,
but he never did. All along, I thought you were
depressed. All along, you were slipping away,
deeper and deeper.

The day no one could find you, I walked around
all day praying to God that you were alive.
I will forever save the text you sent me back
saying that no one can help you. We have all felt
that way in our lives, but now I know you see
that you are with the people who will help you
and have helped so many people before you.

All the stories, the stealing, the lies, the fights,
selling drugs, owing money, and so on, and so
forth. I don't know who that is, and I hope and
pray I never have to. You said it yourself that
I've only seen peeks of the real Mike the last
few years.

We have all as a family put so many things on hold because of you and the disgusting drugs. Your sister has suffered emotionally because we are always focused on helping you and paying attention to you. We have paid thousands of dollars for unused tuition, rent, cars, and paying your friends back. We have not taken vacations, not even been able to buy each other birthday gifts because of what this addiction has cost us. We have all been dragged into this journey as a family and have lost years of our own lives because of it. That's the part of it that I don't understand. I would say to myself, just let him go. He doesn't care about anyone else in this family, and we will lose everything we've worked our whole lives for. How can my own son not care?

I was so sick of listening to you talk about how you always help your friends and buy them presents, while you never even sent Dad or me a birthday card for the last two years. Taking drugs to make Mikey feel good but not caring about how anyone else feels. I've watched people I know turn their backs on their children for just these reasons. Written them out of their lives for good, and I could never understand how a mother or father could do that. I understand now.

It's about saving yourself.

Do you think I could never be one of those mothers? Laying in a hospital bed wondering if I was going to die helped me figure all that out. I refuse to let your addiction kill you.

I refuse to let your addiction kill *me*.

We have all started the healing process right along with you. You are the lucky one that has the opportunity to be helped by professionals and are there because you want to be. I am so proud of you for that, and that is why we are with you every step of the way. If you were not committed to this, nothing else would matter.

You are my baby boy and I love you. You have your entire life ahead of you, and I cannot wait for you to start living it. We will all be here for you, holding you up every step of the way. I love you, Mikey, and I have incredible faith in you. Please come back to us. I miss you more than you will ever know.

Mom

CHAPTER 9

I CAN REMEMBER

Anita

I wrote my second cost letter to Mike once I returned from his house in Vermont. I keep being told that addiction is not about me, me, me, or anyone else in the family. Honestly, I think that's a lot of bullshit. My next letter expresses how I felt after walking into that house and seeing exactly how my son was living. My eyes were wide open for the first time, and I honestly was happy to have the opportunity to tell Mike how I really felt while he was in treatment. I felt that he would be able to work through it with his team at Caron, and I was grateful for my friend Margie, who took me to my first Al-Anon meeting so I could start to work through it all myself.

I reached out to friends who had gone through this with their own kids. I reached out to a lot of different people to try and understand how to get past the things I couldn't handle. I realized that so many people who have either gone through treatment or have someone in their family who has, all deal wih it in their own way. There is no one right way to help yourself. I only know that no matter which way you find help, you cannot stop until you do. You cannot go through it alone. You cannot begin to understand what or how to help someone until you understand the illness and help yourself as well. It was time to educate myself with anything I could get my hands on.

I reached out to one of Mike's counselors and explained how I was afraid to write the things I really wanted to say in my next letter to him. I was angry, really angry. I didn't want to knock him down when he was trying so hard to get back up already. I was told to write the truth, no matter how bad. The lies could not continue for any of us, and he needed to hear how I really felt. So I did.

Mike,

I wrote you my first letter the day after we dropped you off at Caron, feeling scared and sad and uncertain of the future. I am writing you now filled with nothing but disbelief, anger, and disgust. Your lies leading up to entering Caron, even on the day before, have been nothing short of a nightmare. Although your father has always chosen to believe in you, I have had many doubts and have now been proven correct. I will not blame myself anymore, because none of this could have taken place until you reached the point you did last week. I wonder how much longer you could have gone on with your schemes and lies and the other life you were living. I feel so terribly sad for the boys you lived with in Vermont after going there yesterday. I don't know how they let you enter their house on a daily basis. I don't know how I did either.

After going to Vermont, I have done *nothing* but sort through your bags of garbage. Throwing away and washing. Throwing away and washing. Clothes of a bum. Everything is filthy and every pocket has remnants of drug paraphernalia. Pot seeds, broken pills, foil, plastic bags, lighters, matches, and so much more. All the time telling me you had no money in your possession. Lie. Actually everything you told me was a big bag of lies.

Once Dad and I dropped you off at Caron, we drove back home exhausted, and although we both collapsed, neither of us could sleep. We couldn't sleep because we were worried about you. We are both having nightmares, throwing up, and crying 24-7 ever since Dad picked you up last week. You look nothing like the photos

I have of you around the house. You look like a
strung out, filthy, skinny punk.

I went to Vermont yesterday through a blizzard
to get up to your house and clean up your mess.
Upon entering your room, I threw up. Instead
of walking into a college son's room and finding
girl's phone numbers and books, I was a mother
walking into a drug den. The only books and
numbers in that shit hole were ones with notes
from people asking you to hook them up. Wow
Mike. How cool you must have been driving
around in Mom's car, dealing drugs. Yet you
were calling me every chance you had asking
for money for skiing and books. Lies. All lies.
Burlington police violations, emergency room
bills, broken furniture everywhere. Good old
Mikey...doesn't give a crap about anyone but
himself. The saddest part of all was when I
stood in the middle of this chaos and asked
myself, "Who lives in this room? Where are my
son's things?" We found them in the basement
covered in dust. Remnants of the person we had
dropped off to college packed away. I am still
unpacking bags and boxes, afraid to look inside.

I couldn't get out of there fast enough, Mike. I
was told by your roommates they would have
called me sooner but were afraid to because

you told them I was dying after having a heart attack. "Very touch and go," you would tell everyone so that they would feel bad for you and not call us. This alone sickens me the most.

Somehow your paperwork was overlooked, and you were not processed to be thrown out of school. Dropping from a fantastic GPA, we now could see when this all started to happen. After paying for a semester that we pulled you out of on a medical emergency for your so-called depression, you spiraled downward. After spending thousands of dollars on you for help and care, you still went on to let us pay for another semester and rent. Withdraw and fail. Withdraw and fail. Another proud moment for your parents. All the while your father is getting up at 6:00 a.m., going to work to pay for your education. After paying for four years of college, you are only halfway done, and we are on the verge of losing everything.

Thank you, Mike. Thanks for nothing. That's all you've done for the past two years of your young life. Nothing. You lay in bed all day doing drugs. What a great visual for a mother to have. Just when I think I couldn't be any less proud, you prove me wrong.

Your lies, drug use, and manipulation have
affected so many people I cannot even begin
to count. I will not be coming to see you on
visitation days. I will not be coming until I
am told I have to. I am tired, and my soul is
broken. Just like everyone else in this family.

Mom

Mike had been at Caron for about two weeks before
we would go up for the family part of treatment. I chose
not to visit him on Sunday visitation days because I simply didn't want to. I didn't even want to go for family
time in a few weeks, but I knew I had to. I was angry
that now we had to pay for my poor daughter to fly in,
pay someone to stay with our dog, and Michael had to
take time off from work again. That's how mad I was at
this point. I was so sick of it all.

We drove to Pennsylvania again to my godparents'
house, and Alex flew in from LA. We all had dinner
together that night, and my godparents told us about
their visits with Mike on the previous Sundays. I could
tell how much they believed in him and his recovery,
and I could tell they felt needed, which made them
happy. My godfather seemed to have gotten very close
with my son and wanted to be a part of his life moving
forward. He said he felt like a grandfather for the first
time and that if Mike wanted to stay with them once he
finished treatment that they wanted to have him.

We woke very early the next morning and headed back up that big hill to Caron. I wondered how my son was going to react to us since we had just sent him the letters, which we knew he had read.

We would be going to classes and lectures for two days before even seeing my son. The most important part of this training for me was the medical lectures. I never, ever believed that addiction was a disease.

I always felt that addiction was a choice. Addiction was an excuse.

As I sat there listening to doctor after doctor talk about addiction, I couldn't get past the anger of being stuck in that lecture hall learning about something I had no desire to learn about and taking time away from our lives again because of my son doing drugs. I felt like I was on a poorly made after-school movie. All the words they were using made me nauseous while describing the types of drugs and how they rewire your brain. I was having a very hard time getting past the anger to the point where I could actually listen and try and understand what was happening with my son. No matter how much information I was given, I still questioned what had been so bad or wrong in his life for him to start doing drugs.

I finally connected to one of the people speaking, when through the fog I heard a lecturer ask all of us, "How many of you right now are not listening to me but asking yourself, 'Why my son or daughter? What was so bad in their life that made them start doing drugs?'"

This was a turning point for me. I was finally listening to someone who knew exactly how I felt. I could see every other parent start to sit up and listen as well at the same time. This room filled with tired, worn-down parents who all looked just like us. Was there hope? Was someone going to give me the answers I'd been searching for all along? Was this person going to explain what I had done wrong? Would it be something I could fix myself and take my son home and it would all be OK? Instead he showed us on a big-as-life screen what happens to your brain if you have the disease of addiction. I could relate to it, being a smoker most of my life, and the way this man was explaining everything was actually really interesting.

My son has explained to me that whether or not it's alcohol or drugs, the reason one is an addict is because when everyone else stops partying on Sunday night and goes back to class on Monday morning, an addict cannot. Now this guy was explaining why. For the first time at the end of that day, I started to understand and believe that addiction is a disease. It also made me a little more nervous, wondering how my son's brain was ever going to be normal again. Was he up to this daunting task? There was no surgery for this illness. There was only a lot of hard work and the desire to change. I was cautiously optimistic. Only time would tell.

I was getting more and more anxious about seeing him for the first time. My husband and daughter were excited and hopeful. I, sadly, didn't feel that way.

I didn't trust my son anymore and wondered if I ever would again.

Sunday morning, we were all led into a very large nondenominational church on the Caron grounds. I wondered why there were so many boxes of tissues everywhere in the aisles, under the seats, everywhere. The church was filled with families waiting to see their sons and daughters, filled with excitement as if they were at a debutante ball waiting for the "coming out." My husband and daughter felt the same way and kept turning around, waiting to see my son walk through the door. I was shaking. I was still angry, still filled with hate.

There were a few rows of kids who looked just like Mike did the day we dropped him off. They looked tired, disheveled, and weren't paying attention to anyone.

A man named Father B took to the pulpit. First, he spoke to the group of young people who had just started at Caron. There was something about the way he spoke that made me very calm. There was no anger, no disappointment. In every word you could feel how much he cared for these kids and their well-being. He was a wonderful man, and he made me feel terrible for feeling the way I did.

After he finished addressing the kids who were just starting out, different groups of kids started getting up and reciting poems, reading letters, singing, or just telling their story.

Ten seconds into the first young man speaking, I understood what the boxes of tissues were for. From the moment he opened his mouth, I couldn't stop crying. Father B introduced each one as if they were his own child and stood beaming with pride as he listened to them.

Then he announced there would be a group joining us that was halfway through their stay at Caron, and my heart almost jumped out of my body. That was my son's group.

What would he look like? Would he look the same as when we brought him here? Would he ask to come home with us? He had let me down so much for so long that I prayed I wouldn't grab him by the throat. I prayed I wouldn't lose my cool and make a scene in front of all those people, in front of Father B.

Alex was the first to see him. Her face erupted into a huge smile, tears rolling down her face "There he is!" she said.

I didn't turn to look at my son. I looked at my daughter. I couldn't understand how she was so happy to see him while I didn't even want look at him. After all he had put her through, here she was, a proud, emotional, joyous sibling. My daughter looked so beautiful and innocent at that moment.

I was in awe.

Alex

I didn't know what to expect when we got to the rehab, but I was oddly excited knowing that I was going to see my brother. He had written me a letter a few days before

I arrived in Pennsylvania, and he sounded good. I was curious to see how much he had changed. I was also nervous because I knew he had read my cost letter. I didn't want him to think that I hated him. I wanted him to know that I was making an effort to repair whatever was left of our relationship.

The first day, Saturday, was a lot of lectures. We were with the other "young adult" parents in a room with a speaker, preparing for what would happen when we saw our family member. I looked around the room a few times and realized to my surprise that I was the only sibling.

On Sunday we had to go to church with the rest of the parents and kids in the rehab. I was told the day before that it was an extremely powerful and emotional ceremony, especially because it's the first time you see your family member. I was so sick the entire morning waiting to see Mike. Sitting in the church waiting for him to come in felt like forever, when it was really only forty-five minutes.

I remember my dad just had a quiet, reserved, thoughtful look on his face. It was the same face he had at his best friend Tommy's funeral, who had died on 9/11. It was also the same face he had at my uncle Gary's funeral, who had died on 9/11. He was so sad that all of this was happening, yet he was so hopeful that it would all turn out all right for Mike. I could tell he was scared and asking himself if this was his fault. It wasn't. It wasn't anyone's fault but Mike's.

My mom looked so nervous. Her fists were clenched, and I thought she might punch Mike in the face when he walked in. She had been through it all with Mike and this was her time to really express how she felt and let it all come out. My mom is the glue that holds our family together. In fact she holds most people's lives together. Whenever something was wrong with anyone, my mom found the fastest way to fix it and just did it. Never complained, never thought about it. She just fixed it. She had tried so hard to fix Mike, but she knew when she dropped him off at the rehab that he was the only one that could fix him.

Mike walked in, and we just stared at each other for a moment, and his face lit up. It was the most honest, healthy, and happy Mike I had ever seen in my life. We embraced, and I felt like we were hugging each other for the first time.

We listened to a few of the addicts speak to their families, read letters, or play music for a bit, and then Mike stood up to speak. I was shocked. I was even more shocked when he asked Mom, Dad, and me to go up to the podium and stand with him in front of the entire church. Mike read the most beautiful letter he had written, which reflected that he was finally ready to start being a part of this family. I was on board if he was.

The entire day was filled with communication-type exercises to help each family really express how they felt. I really found the entire process quite useful, and I definitely spoke more than anyone else, which isn't

uncommon for me. During the lunch break, I took
Mike aside and talked to him privately for a bit. I wanted to really look at him and hear how he felt to try and
understand what he was going through. I left nothing
unsaid. I told him that I would support any decisions he
made as long as he was sober. I also told him that if he
continued to hurt our family, strip us of our happiness,
and take everything our parents worked so hard for that
we were finished. I made it very clear that I would no
longer be a part of his life, and I meant it. I would have
to walk away. The look in his eyes when he promised me
that he would be OK was different than it was that past
Christmas. *This* time it was the look of faith and hope
and strength. He told me that my letter was the most
powerful one he had read, and I believed him. Most important, I wanted to help him. My brother spent his
twenty-second birthday at Caron. I couldn't believe he
was twenty-two and sober.

Anita

Next I watched my husband do exactly the same thing.
He was just as happy, just as excited to see Mike as Alex
had been. I thought back to what my husband had written in his cost letter to Mike.

Dear Mike,

When a Man bears a son, a certain bond seems
to immediately take hold. As a father you want

to take that boy and teach him everything
you know and raise him with some of the
same experiences that you experienced. That is
exactly what I wanted to do for you, and that is
the kind of relationship that I wanted for you
and me. We have had a good bond through
the years, but I know that it was tough for you
when I wasn't around during the week when
I was working in the city. However, when you
started taking up lacrosse, I felt that we had
something together that we could share. Your
competitiveness and your desire to be better
were really things that made me proud as a
father, and I wanted to watch those qualities
grow. You became quite a good player, and I
was so happy to watch your progress and be
there for you.

I have always tried to be a good father and role
model, but I am far from perfect, and I know
that I embarrassed you a few times with my
overexuberance on the lacrosse field. You also
grew up in a family environment that was quite
large and one that enjoyed a good time with the
pleasures of alcohol. Whether that has anything
to do with your current situation is unknown,
but it is something for us, as a family, to bear
in mind.

Obviously your situation was a mystery to
us for quite some time. You always seemed
to do all right in high school as far as grades
go, but your attitude was changing and that
was something that was disturbing. You were
growing older and wanted to be your own man,
so I just let it be, but there was something else
going on that we would not find out about
for some time. We began fighting more and
disagreeing about your path for the future and
a tension started to emerge in our relationship.
At times I wasn't really sure who I was talking
to and the lack of respect toward both your
mother and me was horrifying. I knew you were
on some kinds of drugs but never realized it
had escalated as far as it had.

Mike, I love you and will always try to take care of
you. However there has been some serious damage
done to many of your relationships. You have
put up a good front for some of your more casual
relationships, like our friends or some of your
aunts, uncles, and cousins, but the real hurt is
your immediate family. Your sister, mother, and I
have endured a couple of years of worry, pain, and
suffering. I've worried for years that you would do
something to hurt yourself. You would call and
tell me that you needed this or that, and I would

get off the phone not either knowing or believing what you were telling me. All of this scared me to death, and the more I gave to you, the less I got back. Then last year when you finally came clean and asked for help, I began to think that everything was going to be OK, and it seemed OK, but only for a short period of time.

This past summer when you came to live with us for the break, I thought we would have a great time, but it turned out to be a big nightmare. I was as angry with you this summer as I had ever been in your life. You were a shell of the man I raised, and I could not believe what I was watching. You had no ambition and no sense of who you were. You slept days away and could not finish even the most menial jobs. You even wanted to join the Coast Guard as a means to escape. I was scared for you and felt I was losing my son. There seemed to be nothing I could say to make things right, and I was fearful that we were losing you. Mike, I never want that to happen, and I never want to have that feeling again. I want the Mike that I know to come out and show his true self. I want the fire and competiveness and the will to excel to once again be the most important thing in your life. You have so many great qualities and a life that is just starting. Use those qualities to make things better in your life and others' lives. You have more to give than you will ever know. Love yourself, and I want you to want to stop hurting the ones who love you the most.

I will love you forever, Dad

Anita

"I see him," Michael said, crying and smiling, just like Alex.

I felt abandoned. I felt alone.

Why are they so happy? Why am I the only one filled with anger? Have they already forgotten why we are all here? When I finally turned to look for Mike, I was holding onto that anger as tight as I could. I wouldn't be so easily fooled as the rest of my family, I thought.

But then I saw him.

As he walked toward us, I started to shake. The person we had dropped off a few weeks ago was nowhere in sight. Before me was the son I had not seen for years. How could this physical change happen so quickly? He looked healthy and happy, and for the first time in a long time, his beautiful eyes were back. We all hugged each other, and he sat down between my daughter and my husband. I was happy he hadn't sat down next to me. I just wanted to sit in silence and observe.

I watched the group Mike had come in with go up to the podium. Each one took turns telling their story. I assumed Mike wasn't going to because he didn't like to speak in front of crowds. They were almost to the last person when Mike got up and walked over to the front of the church. What happened next is something I will never forget as long as I live and will remember as one of my proudest moments as a mother.

When the last person in the group finished speaking, Father B got up and asked everyone to listen to the next speaker, no matter what they were doing.

"Hearing what this young man says is important. To all of us." I felt like he was looking directly at me. Before he introduced Mike, he said he knew right away Mike wanted to be there. He knew Mike wanted help and had been working very hard and that he knew his words were going to have an impact on everyone there.

When I saw my son walk up there, I heard the women in front of us talking about how handsome he was. I had no idea what was going to happen next. Mike asked for his family to join him on the altar while he read something he had written. All three of us stood and walked awkwardly to the front of the church. Father B motioned for us to stand with Mike at the podium.

I was a wreck and just wanted the whole thing to be over with. But then Mike started to speak.

Mike

I was so on board with the family program at Caron and looked forward to it. I felt that the only way to find freedom was to be honest with them. And I was excited to see my family. I felt so many things seeing them for the first time, but joy stood out the most. This was the first time I felt that way in a long time. I had the piece of paper in my pocket with what I wrote the night before, unsure as to whether or not I would actually make it to the podium to actually read it aloud. I let every other speaker get up before me. When it came to the end, I felt as if someone grabbed me by the shoulders and put me up in the front of the chapel. I was terrified to read this out loud, but as my family came up and stood beside me, I felt a sudden rush of comfort and closeness to them.

I began to read the following.

I can remember being young and free,
without a care in the world. The world as my
playground, and my Big Wheel as my vessel
through life. I can remember the warmth
of heart from my mother and father as they
carried me on this journey. I can remember this
felt good.

I remember vacations with my family.
Wherever we wanted to go, and together, we
did it. Trips to Florida, the Bahamas—you
name it, I remember. They all felt good.

I remember playing lacrosse. My family and
friends coming to watch me play. The wins,

the goals, the great feeling of support and accomplishment. All of it felt good.

I remember going away to college. The loss of friends, the loss of lacrosse, and the loss of my sense of place and direction. I can remember this felt…not so good.

I remember giving up. Giving in to all the wrong things that made me feel good. That took away the pain and made me feel happy again. I guess this felt good.

Now, all I can remember is pain. The lies, the stealing, the manipulation, ignorance, and selfishness. I remember spending every cent, selling everything, and asking for more from others who had nothing to give. I can remember feeling nothing at all.

I can remember making my mother cry, my sister hide, and my father feel helpless. Making those who loved me become full of anger and disgust toward me. I can remember the vacations disappeared, my family and everything I loved slowly moving in the same direction. This didn't feel good at all.

I do remember the feeling of hope though. That support and love of my family still lingered beneath the surface of all that pain. They're still here, and they want me back. They want back what I've hid from them and what I've taken away from them. Is that too much to ask? Why are we so afraid of feeling good again? What is so scary about life and feeling that warmth we've all known?

I can feel the hope build and the warmth rise. I can actually feel again. I can remember. There is progress to be made and steps to take, but I believe we can all still live a life that everyone will want to remember.

Anita

I remember standing up there with everyone staring at us, not knowing what to feel. But when he got to the fourth and fifth paragraphs, something clicked inside of me. His loss of friends. He had lost a lot of friends to drugs and suicide, even while in high school. He never handled death well and why should he have been expected to at such a young age?

His loss of lacrosse. I felt a pang of guilt because he had been asked to play lacrosse for Springfield and I was the one that pushed him to go to UVM. He ended up having two surgeries before his freshman year started and never made it onto the field.

Did my control issues play a part of the direction he had headed in? Would he have been happier at Springfield College? I knew why I had pushed him to go to Vermont, but did he hate me for it? I was quite certain he did. I would have if I were him.

After the ceremony, we were going to sit down alone with Mike for the first time since he'd come to Caron, and I was afraid to hear what he really thought of me. I was afraid to hear a lot of things.

Alex wanted to see Mike first. She would be going back to California in a few short days, so it was important for her to have as much alone time with him as possible. I couldn't hear their conversation, but I distinctly remember the expression on their faces as they talked to each other over the table.

Alex looked like a mom talking to Mike. She was very serious yet caring. No matter what she was saying to him, it looked as if her message was, "I'm here for you and love you, but this is it."

I could tell she was proud of him. She wanted her little brother back. That's all she ever wanted. Mike was listening intently, taking in every word she was saying. I saw it in his eyes. He understood.

It was one of the most touching moments I've seen between my two children. He knew how much he hurt her. He also knew she was one of the only siblings that had come to this family week. When Alex unleashed her emotions, she held nothing back. Her pain was released through each word she spoke. I could feel it from across the room. Seeing her get through, and seeing them be brother and sister again washed away my fear of talking to my son. I spied on them for a few more minutes and then reported back to my husband, who was already making friends with some of the other fathers in our group.

When Alex and Mike rejoined us, I didn't say much and let Michael do most of the talking. I just found myself staring at my son. Seeing him healthy and calm, so very different from the monster I had been used to these last few years. I tried to soak it all in just in case it didn't last.

I was afraid to be hopeful. The day was filled with beautiful stories and uplifting prayers and honest talks. Yet I was still filled with hate and anger.

I thought I was the only one smart enough to think that this could all be a new form of manipulation. When I started to believe I was wrong, and there was reason to be hopeful, it pissed me off how, in only two short weeks, these strangers helped my son in ways I wasn't able to in the past few years.

Looking around, I seemed to be the only one who felt this way. And that made me even angrier, which was something I didn't think was possible.

CHAPTER 10

FINDING MY FAITH

Anita

As scary as the idea was, I was looking forward to family therapy. I didn't want to feel like this anymore. I had to be honest with everyone, including myself, and give the program a chance if I wanted to start to heal. I was ready. I was tired of being mad. I was ready to let it all out. I was ready to be attacked. I also found it hard to believe that anyone could help me.

We were put in groups of six families. When we all settled in and introduced ourselves, I was surprised at what I saw. Sitting shoulder to shoulder were lawyers, deans of schools, medical professors, men and women from upper-class families. The stigma that drug addicts only come from lower class families was shattered. Looking around, I started to feel less alone.

I listened intently as one of the boys talked about how his coach had supplied pain pills to his high school team to play better.

Every parent in that room cringed.

The mothers and fathers in the room had the same lost look on their faces as Michael and I did. They had all believed, just as we had, that something like this could never happen to their child. Just like us, they were realizing that just because their kids were athletes, just because they were popular and good looking and went to private schools didn't mean they weren't in danger of developing a very ugly drug problem.

I was very surprised that Alex was the only sibling in the room. We found out later that some of the siblings were much younger and had gone into a different group with other counselors because they were too young to handle the exercises our group was about to go through.

The next exercise took place in a room that had different emotions written on the walls. We were told to stand under the sign which best expressed how we felt at the time. I walked around looking for the right word. I passed my husband, who had stopped in the "sad"☹ corner, and my son in the "joyous"☺ corner. I passed "confused," "fearful," and "worried" until I saw where I belonged.

I was standing alone in the "angry" corner.

I think the rest of my family was embarrassed, but I didn't care.

The next few days consisted of trust exercises. We traded kids and went one-on-one with each other. We listened to the timelines of our children's drug use, how and when it escalated, and the near overdoses.

The kids wanted to tell us everything. They didn't want to hide any of it. It poured out of them. It was so hard to listen to, but we were learning how to trust them again. Listening when they wanted to talk was the first step.

I listened to how wrong I had been about so many things.

By now, I was way past the point of thinking that a beautiful house, a private school and a country club could keep your kids clean. Looking around this room of brokenhearted parents, I understood. All of us had given too much to our children, especially too much money. Money was what paid for these expensive drugs. Money we handed out to our kids because we wanted them to be happy. Money they used to try and kill themselves.

I sucked in all the information I could. I listened to my son talk about how it all had progressed. I listened to the other kids and watched how some parents reacted. I realized how up to this point I had made this situation to be so much about me, me, me, and now finally realized it was all about Mike. He was the one that had to do all the work.

I started to fantasize about the future. I thought he would finish his thirty days and come home to start his new life, all fixed like the car I had dropped off for a tune-up.

What would it be like to have him be part of our family again? I thought about him going to ball games with my husband and having dinner as a family. I felt jealous of everyone at Caron who was spending time with him as this new person. I wanted that relationship with him, but I knew I had to stop being an overbearing mother. He needed my encouragement and support, not my judgment. I knew I needed to work out my anger if I was ever going to be able to help my son.

I didn't care what it took. I was ready to go to Al-Anon and therapy and ready to be a better mother. I needed to be a mother who would let her son breathe and grow up. I needed to be a mother who didn't have a joint bank account with her son. I needed to be a mother who didn't try to fix everything whenever it went wrong.

Most of all, I was looking forward to being a wife who would never hide anything from my husband about his son again.

I had to change. I had been a part of the problem, and I wanted a chance to be who I needed to be for my son to stay on this new path. Was I still angry? Absolutely. But I sat with the counselors one-on-one and talked about how mad I was for the financial situation and Mike's part in it. They asked me if I talked to our kids about it, and my answer was yes. Why wouldn't I explain to them that we were not in a position to help them financially? Why wouldn't I share with them why

I was so stressed out all the time? I felt they needed to understand and that they were old enough to hear it.

When asked again how I had been handling the stress myself, I told them about my heart attack.

"If that's what happened to you, how do you think your kids can handle the information?" the counselors asked. "You don't need to put that stress on either of them because it doesn't help the situation, it doesn't make things better, and now they are worried about their parents on top of it all. It's not as if they're in a position to help."

It was a slap in the face. One I wished I'd had years ago.

One of the most important parts of the thirty days at Caron was learning how to be a better parent. It was not about sitting down and whining and complaining about our lives. It's not about what's best for Mom or Dad or the one in treatment. It's about everyone and the work that needs to be done to bring us all back together.

I had to stop treating Mike like he was still a little boy. I needed to trust that he would make good decisions. We are the ones that found Caron, but Mike made the decision to go. Mike made the decision to stay there. Mike made the decision to do whatever had to be done to get healthy.

Mike was also the one who made the decision not to come home after his stay at treatment was done. He is the one who made the decision not to be on the East Coast right after leaving Caron. He made the decision that he couldn't be around the people who would make him weak and not to jump back into the codependent relationship he had with his mother. He wanted to go to a sober living community in Dallas, Texas, for a few months.

I wanted to explode.

What the fuck? Does he hate us that much that he's afraid to come home? I was raging, and I realized that no matter how much I thought I had changed, I still wanted control. I called his counselor at Caron, who told me that he agreed with Mike. Mike wanted to continue on his path to be drug-free. He wanted to put more time into changing his behavior and to put more distance between his past and who he was now.

I liked Mike's counselors and respected them. They took a lot of time to call us and asked us to talk about ourselves, how we were feeling, and how we were doing. We would also write to each other, and they were always available for anything we wanted to talk about. I loved Mike's personal counselor, Rob. He was a gentle soul who put up with a lot of crap from me and still continued to answer my calls. But I was furious that he was agreeing with Mike about going to Dallas to a sober living place called the Gaston House. Why couldn't he come home?

I researched the Gaston House and had no problem picking up the phone and calling the director/owner who runs the program. As the daughter of a Greek Orthodox priest, I panicked when I read about the theological instruction at this place. Of course I was thinking, "Now that he's off drugs, will he become addicted to some radical Bible study?" I called Mr. West that day and bombarded him with a hundred questions. I remember telling him, "Don't think for a minute that you are going to turn my son into a Bible thumper! You are not going to pull my son into some kind of religious cult!" Much to my amazement, he remained calm with me on the phone.

I didn't trust him even so. I didn't trust any of it. My son was getting on a plane and going there no matter what I thought. I was scared. I was mad that he wasn't coming home. I was also mad that I had to figure out how to pay for the next three months of this program. I also had to make yet another appeal to our insurance company for reimbursement for the rehab.

After years of paying into this medical plan and submitting all the mounds of evidence and letters from doctors, it was apparent that this program had saved his life. It was apparent to everyone but the insurance company. They still claimed that Mike never needed to be in a rehab.

Why was I so afraid of Mike having religion in his life? Was it because I had lost my faith along the way?

I had not been to church since my father had died years earlier. At that point in my life, I wasn't clear about what I should actually have faith in.

No matter what I said or thought, Mike was off to Dallas straight out of rehab. A few weeks had passed when I received this first letter from Mike.

Mom,

For the first time in my life, I feel like I truly
am becoming my own man. I have grown a
lot in these few weeks, and I feel as though
our family is stronger than ever. For years my
addiction and discomfort has created so much
stress and worry in the family. Finally, with
the help of you, Dad, and Alex, we have been
able to break my spell. You have given me an
opportunity to see where I can grow and how to
apply it to my own life.

You may wonder why I couldn't do that in
the past. The answer is that I don't know the
reason why. All I know is that I'm doing it
now. I am growing as you and Dad always
wanted me to. I am learning to do the things
I need to do to survive and covering my own
tracks myself.

My family is the number-one thing I have in
my life, and I would never want things to go
back to the way they were before. We've always
talked about my issue of never being able to
stay in one place and growing. I always jump
around with inconsistency and quit everything.
That is the part where I fail to grow.

I have fears about coming back to the East
Coast just as I'm beginning to build some
consistency. It's not that I'm afraid that I'll
use drugs. I want to get out of the habit of
bouncing around. My biggest fear is to come
back and become too dependent on you and
Dad again.

I never want you guys to worry and stress
because of me manipulating your trust ever
again. I want to be able to give back for all you
have done for me and for everything I've put
you through.

Mom, there is no telling what is to come in
the upcoming months. Yet, I still have no
reservations. I write this to you because I want
to be able to openly talk about everything
when the time comes. I still take it one day at
a time; however, the future is inevitable. For
it is not what we do but how we do it and the
motivation and intentions behind our decisions
that define us.

I love my family more than anything in the
world, Mom. I only want the best for our
family. You and Dad and Alex have done so
much for me, and it's time you get something

back. You are persistent, strong willed, open minded, and have a huge heart. You are always willing to go the extra mile for anyone that is willing to go with you, yet you take shit from no one. I'm proud to be a son with a mother I can look up to. I love you, Mom. Thank you for never giving up on me.

Love always,
Your son,
Mikey

Mike

When I first got to the Gaston House in Dallas, I was very excited. I was ready to meet new people, go to work, and start living. I knew it was a good idea to have distance from home so that I could live as an independent, mature man. It also put distance between me and my familiar environment. I didn't know what would come next. All I knew was that I was ready to follow any direction that was given to me.

The first week there, I found an opportunity to coach lacrosse. One of my counselors had suggested it as something I would be good at, and so I got on the computer to search for a lax job. As I started looking, I had a familiar feeling of shame. I had walked away from lacrosse in college and felt I may be judged by my fellow coaches. I would think of myself as a failure in their eyes, and then my own. This is when I realized something in me had changed. I didn't let fear threaten me or control my actions. I shot out as many e-mails and made as many phone calls as I could that day. Instead of running away, I pushed forward.

The following week I started coaching for a middle school youth lacrosse team.

In the beginning, I was nervous of how I would perform. I wanted to look good as a coach. I wanted people to respect me. When I opened up about this to a counselor, he made me realize I was thinking selfishly.

He asked me why I was going out there. Was I going out there to look good and build up my ego, or was I going out there to be as helpful as I possibly could? He told me one simple thing. I should remove myself from the equation and ask how I could be of utmost service to others.

Exposing my feelings was important to me because it helped me find new solutions. Each uncomfortable feeling I had always led to me getting loaded. It was a surefire way to cover up those feelings. Now, instead of avoiding them, I was discovering new ways to deal with my emotions.

My life had gone from robbing my friends and sleeping at homeless shelters to riding a bus in Dallas, Texas, between three different jobs. I was still going to shelters, but for an entirely different reason: to help feed the homeless or to speak to them about getting sober and to tell my story.

The first few months at Gaston were a breeze, but then one day, a waterfall of emotion came pouring out of me. Even though I thought I had come so far, I was still not dealing with things way down inside of me. My mentor, Chico, has a good acronym for this mixture of feelings: S-O-B-E-R.

"Son of a bitch—everything's real."

Just because I wasn't doing drugs anymore didn't mean I was an expert at dealing with my feelings. I had to learn to constantly expose what was going on inside of me to be completely free of my illness. I was afraid to look like a coward, so I continued to keep my feelings inside. I knew that exposing feelings was good just as long as it wasn't "me" exposing my feelings. But I have to continuously remember that it's not my actions that are my problem. It is my mind that needs healing. Everything else comes later.

After overcoming this first rough patch, I was excited that my sister was coming to Dallas. I was really looking forward to spending some time with her.

Alex

I visited Mike in Texas a few months after he had moved there. I wanted to see how he was doing, see his life, and see how much had changed. His bad attitude had vanished. There was no more lying and sneaking around. There was no more ignoring him when he called, and most important, I wanted to be a part of his life.

Mike and I are still repairing our relationship day by day. There is no quick fix for something like this, and I will always remember this time of my life. It has made me so much stronger and made me really grow up. It also made me realize that no family is perfect, and we should appreciate the ones we have.

I am still working on forgiving my brother. Only now, I respect him. I brag about him. I am proud of him. The family therapy at Caron brought our family closer together than we have ever been before. And for that, I will always be grateful to my brother.

Anita

I called Alex as soon as she got back from her trip to Dallas. I wanted to know how Mike was doing from someone who wasn't him.

After hearing her gush about how Mike had changed, I knew I needed to apologize to Chico West for the way I had spoken to him. I wrote him a letter explaining my fears when Mike told me he was going to Dallas. I told him everything I was feeling, revealing a lot of secret thoughts a mother usually keeps in the vault.

Most important, I thanked him.

I thanked him for helping Mike step back into life after leaving treatment. As mad as I had been in the beginning, it was the first step toward trusting Mike to make good decisions. I was proud of him. I was grateful he had this wonderful man as a mentor in his new life, a man who selflessly spends his life helping boys who are trying to help themselves.

Mike never asked for anything while in Dallas. He was not the spoiled, entitled kid I had created anymore. He was working three jobs, going to meetings, and riding the bus for hours every day to get to where he needed to be. Gone were the days of driving around a Range Rover that his parents paid for and asking for money to put gas in it. He was working hard and earning everything on his own. He was becoming his own man, just as he had said in his letter.

Michael and I loved talking to him and hearing about everything he was doing. He had walked away from lacrosse and was now getting back involved as a coach. It was always his passion, and now he was sharing it with kids.

Michael, Alex, and I knew that Mike was on his way to being happy.

We all wanted him to finish school, but it would have to happen on Mike's terms. He knew we would not be paying for any more schooling, and he would be responsible for tuition. He also knew he had to buy his own car. It felt good to let him be his own man. I think it made him feel even better.

Did my baby boomer generation hand too much to their kids? Did making them feel privileged and entitled hurt them more than help them? I questioned everything I had done in the interest of being a good parent. It would have never occurred to me to make my son ride the bus everywhere when I could afford to give him a car. It would never have occurred to me that denying him would be helping him. Even now, as I learn to accept the new dynamic of my family, it's still hard not to want to fix everything all the time.

As months went by, things started feeling "normal." Michael and I finally started doing the things empty nesters do. We had been under everyone's looking glass years earlier when we were going through our own troubles. We would constantly hear about "friends" who would talk behind our backs.

It was hard, but I had to ignore the "friends" who were talking crap about my son. The "friends" whose own kids were so messed up but were and still are ignored by their parents. Parents who don't want to deal with it. They were talking about my son. The one who wanted to go to rehab? The one who is sober now? My anger turned to pride.

Our golden years may have been tarnished, but here and there I see some glimmers of light peek through.

CHAPTER 11

INTERNAL STRUGGLES

Anita

I remember the first time I worried about my son using drugs again.

When he first went out to Dallas, he would love to talk to my godparents in Pennsylvania and fill them in on what he was doing. He had gotten very close to my godfather, Al. When Al suffered a heart attack and passed away, instantly I thought, "How am I going to tell Mike?" He had never handled death well.

When his friends passed away, he had dove deeper into drugs to mask the pain he felt. As much as I was working on trusting him, I wasn't sure how he would handle the news. He was very upset when I told him, but the way he spoke about it was different. He was calm and told me he had an amazing support group at the Gaston House. Unlike before, he wanted to talk about it.

I felt like I'd just leapt over another hurdle. I wasn't afraid for him anymore. Mike was different now. He had amazing faith. When we got off the phone, I realized I'd learned something from Mike. Again. Somewhere along the way I had lost my own faith. Mike's peace made me feel its absence.

In the summer of 2011, Mike's best friend Greg was working in New Jersey. He was like the brother Mike never had and always felt like a second son to Michael and I. When I found out that his living situation in New Jersey was terrible, we told him he could stay with us. It was great having him around while we waited for Mike to finish up in Dallas and move back to New York.

Mike had been interviewing over the phone for a job at an architectural school in new york city. My friend Steven was responsible for setting up the series of interviews and was always so supportive of what Mike had gone through.

When Mike came home, it was awesome. He and Greg were living with us, working their jobs, and I loved watching them interact like they had for so many years. It was this peaceful nostalgia that gave me the confidence to plan a trip to California. I wanted to spend some much-needed time with Alex.

I finally felt like I had something to look forward to. I missed Alex, and it had been years since Michael and I had gone on a vacation.

Driving cross-country with Michael and our dog Skilo would be a great adventure. It was something I had never done before, and since I *hate* to fly, this was the perfect plan for me. As Michael and the boys would watch whatever sporting event was on TV, I would close myself in my room and map out our trip. I couldn't wait to see my daughter and the life she had made for herself in California. We were both counting down the days every time we spoke.

As summer turned into the fall and fall into winter, I sensed something changing with Mike and Greg. They didn't want to be in New York anymore. It was expensive, and they wanted a change. Greg didn't love his job, and he missed his family back on the cape. He started looking for a job in Boston.

Mike was more than grateful for what Steven had done for him by helping him get his new job, but he felt like he was missing something. He missed his community in Dallas. He had made great friends there and really liked Dallas.

Even though it made me sad to think of them both leaving, I kept my mouth shut. I loved having Mike and Greg with us. It was a few of the happiest months I had spent in a long time. But it wasn't my decision to make.

Mike got the call from Chico West offering him a job to manage the Gaston House. The same place Mike had gone to after leaving the rehab. Now he was being offered a great apartment and a job working with the young men who were going through what Mike did. I could tell by the way he was talking about it that he'd made up his mind as soon as Chico had offered him the job.

This wasn't about him not wanting to be here with us. He wanted the job.

Mike

After graduating Gaston House in August 2011 and living for a few months with my good friend David, I decided to go to New York City. My best friend, Greg, had already been living with my parents for the past month. Greg and I had always considered each other brothers. We often talked about living together and working together. We had similar dreams about our futures. It seemed like an ideal opportunity to come back to New York City and look for an apartment with Greg while we were working at our own jobs.

Spending time with Greg and my family at this time was great, but something inside of me felt like something was missing. Greg felt the same way. We realized that this may not be the time for our childhood dreams to happen. We've been friends since grammar school and talked about everything.

A year earlier, before moving to the Gaston House as a client, I imagined it to be like a crack den for sober people because of the stigma of what a halfway house was. It couldn't have been more opposite. The house was set up as a fraternity. We even had a family dog,

Johnny Cash, a black Lab/shepherd mix. The house was clean and sunny, and for the most part, everyone was welcoming. People had smiles on their faces. This house provided an opportunity to not only stay sober but to live sober and happy. Drugs had been my solution to the problems I'd had in my mind my whole life. This house provided me with new solutions that would not create destruction in their path. I would now be living with twenty other guys who would be dealing with the same feelings of pain, shame, guilt, loneliness, and anger, but here we could all learn how to deal with these emotions in ways other than turning to drugs and alcohol.

When I first left Dallas and returned to New York, I had a strong feeling that it was not the best decision. I had loved Dallas, and everything that went on there was nothing short of a miracle. However, I sunk into a minor funk while living in an apartment down south. I became lonely and homesick to the point where I did not want to open up and work through my feelings with the friends I had made. I had come so far, and my pride told me that I could handle stuff on my own again and that I didn't need help at this point. I was lying to myself and everyone else when I said the reason I was moving home was to work and return to college to graduate. The truth was that fear had caught up with me, and I was scared. I wanted the warmth and comfort of my parents, and I also did not want the accountability of my friends that I so relied on and cherished for the past year. This choice, which I felt was a bad idea, turned into a lesson that I would learn.

I was presented with an opportunity to work at a college in New York City, for their sustainable design department. I had studied environmental studies in Vermont and had always found a great interest in the field of sustainability and energy. Steven, my mother's friend, had worked for them and put in a great word for me. This played a key role in me receiving this position. My motivation and intentions for leaving Dallas were the real issues. I wanted to escape out of fear but didn't know what the fear was. Chico had always said that fear stood for "Fuck Everything And Run." I could have tried to work through this fear, but my pride drove me to figure it out on my own and trust my own mind again. I would use this opportunity to work at the school as an excuse to leave Dallas and return to New York.

While living in New York, the conditions seemed to be great. I was living with my best friend, I had my family close, and I had a great job. I again began to believe that what was important were things on the outside. Loneliness and fear followed me to New York from Dallas. I was trying to find an external solution to an internal condition, but I cannot escape my own mind. This loneliness is not the kind where I am by myself and no one is around, but I could in fact be surrounded by twenty people and still feel like I did not belong. It was the kind where I would tell myself that no one would understand, and therefore I am different. This loneliness can lead ultimately to a place of being alone and perhaps back into addiction.

The internal struggle had worsened while living in New York. I did not want to tell anyone because I was afraid I would be viewed as weak. My pride pushed me on, and I hoped everything at some point would feel normal. Motivation and will power became lacking as I began to call in sick to work many times and barely wanted to work when I was there. Again I began to feel as if I was letting people down who had my back and pushed for me because they believed and had faith. Self-pity and remorse crept in, and I could see myself beginning to view myself as a failure once again.

I felt as if I had no one to talk to. I could not just give up and quit this job which had so generously been handed to me. I could not bear to tell my parents, or my best friend, that I wanted to return to Dallas. However, the person I was able to confide in was the very person who had gotten me the job. When I opened up to Steven about how I was feeling, I was completely shocked by his responses. He opened up to me about some of his own struggles, which in many cases were almost identical to my own. He had always told me there was no pressure to push myself into something that I could not handle. He reminded me that I cannot be helpful anywhere else if I did not first find help myself.

I was afraid to share these feelings with my parents for fear that my mother would be angry.

However, by the grace of God, she had already seen my desire to move back to Dallas, and she brought up the topic herself.

Pride, control, and fear had brought me to a place where I could possibly forget all that I had learned. None of us are perfect, and we do not need to be ashamed of who we are. I was reminded that fear, much of the time, is a false belief with an outcome that is usually the opposite of what we fear happening in the first place. I would constantly tell myself that people will hate me, be let down, or even discard me if I feel certain ways. As with Steven, I felt he would be upset because he had gotten me this job. However, he wasn't judgmental, only full of grace and acceptance.

Trusting Steven opened me up once again to be honest about how I felt. I began trusting something greater than me. As I slowly exposed my shortcomings once again, I began to feel a sense of freedom and clarity. I called my friends from Dallas and let them know my thoughts. When I told my best friend, Greg, who I was living with, he opened up and said he wanted to move as well. He was also afraid to tell me because he did not want to upset me. We both had a laugh and felt a sense of complete freedom and peace. There again I had just realized how much we allow our feelings and others' feelings to control our lives and our decisions.

As I began to feel better, it was easier for me to see what path I was to take. It became clearer and clearer.

I shared with others the reasons I moved back to New York and that I was not dealing with what was going on inside me. I realized that I was already where I was meant to be in Dallas and that I had left out of fear.

At the same time, I had received a call from my old boss in Dallas, telling me that one of his employees was leaving and that if I came back, I would have a job. It was as if he knew I was moving back to Dallas. Then the owner of the Gaston House, Chico, told me there was a position open at the sober living house that I went through and that he'd like me to take it.

I wondered if these people knew I was about to return to Dallas. Even my own parents called me out. They had read me and knew I wanted to return to Dallas. They supported any decision I made, and told me that they believed I belonged back there. These were all signs from somewhere about the path I was to take. The importance is not so much in the story but in the lessons that I learned.

While in New York and living on self-will, I began to become mentally and spiritually ill. Resentment, loneliness, and fear ran my life and I was again restless, irritable, and discontent. While I did not get loaded or relapse while there, if I had continued on that path, it would have at some point become inevitable. It became very apparent to me that I am never cured from this illness and that it is never beaten, but I can continue to remain recovered as long as I continue to practice the principles that worked for me.

Moving back to Dallas made me feel guilt and shame with the community I had built down there. I felt as if I had abandoned them. They had helped me through so much and they had become a second family to me. I couldn't understand why I was presented with this opportunity to come back and work for Chico. I couldn't believe how accepting my friends and Chico were of me even to the extent of offering me a job after being gone for three months.

It was the ultimate demonstration of grace towards me. I was extremely grateful to my family for understanding my move and grateful to my community for accepting me back as one of their own. It felt as if I had never left. Even my friend David, who was hurt and felt like I made the wrong choice to come back to New York City in the first place, welcomed me with open arms. It was an exciting opportunity to be working at the place that helped me to become my own man and that I could be a guide and an advocate for the other young men coming into this house.

After all, we can't keep what we don't give away.

Now, back at the Gaston House, I am an advocate, not a client. I looked back on the past year to see how people were most helpful to me so that I could be the same for these guys. Most of my life, people had told me what I needed to do and how I needed to do it, and I felt like they were full of it. When I went to Caron and the Gaston House, I met people who did not tell me what I needed to do. Instead they inspired me by their stories and victories over addiction. These men sparked curiosity and awe in my mind. When I became open to direction, I got help.

I had to trust these men because all of my past ideas had failed to keep me sober.

I had to realize that I cannot tell an individual what is right and what is wrong. I could share my own experiences, and if asked for my direction, I would hand it out freely, just as others had done for me. I learned to trust others by them revealing their innermost selves and me hearing their stories, which were similar to mine, but also by hearing how and why they used drugs. It is easy to tell when a person is truly open and honest because it opens a door through which one can choose to walk or not. This is how I hope to be of service at my new job at the Gaston House for the growth of the young men who would be living there.

Even though relapse is never out of the question for me, or anyone like me, that is not my greatest fear in this life. It is the in-between point that leads to relapse, or perhaps even death. My mind is my problem, and drugs and alcohol were the solution that helped me to feel OK. I began to get a glimpse of the in-between point once again while in New York. It is a lonely and dark place where sometimes death can seem the only, and even best, option. My life is proof that this is not the truth, and that there is always another option. Whether we are drug addicts, alcoholics, or even neither, we all have a mind that can take us to the darkest places of the universe.

We don't need to be afraid to admit these things. It does not make us weak. I used to believe that because I can feel pain or fear that I am weak. That belief is my greatest weakness of all. It takes an exponential amount of courage to admit that I am only a man and to expose these feelings to others, and if I am to grow stronger, for me, this must be done.

After all, we are all only human.

I wrote this letter to my mother before leaving for Dallas. I knew my parents understood, but I felt I needed to write to my mom.

Mom,

These past few months have been some of the best times I have ever had with you and Dad. You say all the time that you finally have your son back, and when I hear that, I am filled with the greatest sense of joy, and it never gets old. I may not show it too often, but I truly feel it. Not only that, but I finally feel like an actual part of this family. I used to feel so alone and like no one understood me, but now I know that you truly understand me. And it's not just the fact that you understand me that feels so peaceful, but it is the amount of strength, effort, and interest that you put forth to understand.

That day in the motel in Vermont, I felt like I had no one. I felt like I was the only person in the world and that no one would care about me. Then I got your text. Yes, I know someone told you to say it, but you took the advice, regardless of how much wreckage I had created. That is what made your love for me so apparent. I knew at that moment that everything would be OK, and I realized that I didn't care if anyone else cared for me just as long as I have my parents and my sister. My life is complete. Oh, and Skilo too.☺

I am so happy that we got to spend time together the past few months. I look back on it all and think about how often we used to fight and try to think about any fights we've had since I've been here. I think it was two or three, which were just my stress of work that we easily resolved each time. Crazy, right? You easily identified what it was that I needed to do to feel better and helped kick me in the butt to jump back into my fellowship up here. You knew what I needed and even though my pride sometimes doesn't like to admit you are right, this time I was able to get over it and admit that you were right.

When I got back into my program, things became simple and enjoyable and most important, my head became clearer. It was as if the conflicting thoughts in my head were cleared out and this allowed me to identify my feelings. It was such a strong feeling that I knew if I kept trying to fight it that I would never stop and that would hinder my ability to be helpful at my job, twelve-step fellowship, and all aspects of my life. I know it must be hard to understand the disease of addiction, but that is where the mental illness plays differently in me than other people. It's like a domino effect, where one thing can affect so many other parts of my life, where fear of disappointing or upsetting others keeps me from following my gut. Before I know it, I have backed myself into a corner.

I am so grateful to have parents that understand and trust my decision. I feel that this is another awesome aspect of our dynamic. It truly takes a huge weight off my shoulders just knowing that I can talk to you about anything at all now.

All these realizations wouldn't be possible without your love, Caron, and the Gaston House. And obviously because of Uncle Nick and Aunt Sophie.

Mom, I am extremely sad to leave because of our relationship now. I hope you understand that I am going back with only the best intentions for my future and our future as a family. You are only as strong as your weakest link, and I know that my mind, body, and spirit will be strongest for my next steps in Dallas. I am going to miss you so much, but I know that this chapter for our family will be one for the records. There is so much going on for all of us right now that I know we will all be able to spread our wings and take flight. We can fly together. We have plenty of time. Even though we are all in different time zones, we are all on a journey together.

I love you and Dad so much that I can't express enough how much I already miss you guys. I am extremely confident that we are on the same path together. Thank you for everything, especially the past year. I am truly grateful to have you and Dad…two parents, two friends that I would do anything for. I know you already have for me. I'll miss you, Mom, and I love you very much.

Love, Mike

CHAPTER 12

THE EVIL EYE

Anita

Mike ended up loving his job at the Gaston House and was very good at it. He was responsible for twenty-one boys at the house, and he also got involved with a new lacrosse company called Sentry Lacrosse. He was managing and coaching and a big part of the new company. It all seemed to make him very happy. Which made me happy.

With Mike in Dallas, I set my sights on California. We left the first week of May and headed to LA to see our daughter. Once we were out there, Mike would be joining us for a week. It would be a real, honest-to-goodness family vacation.

My husband, our dog Skilo, and our nephew Christopher, who had hitched a ride to visit his parents, and I arrived on the fifth day. It wasn't quite the adventure I'd always imagined a cross-country trip would be, but I fell in love with California the moment I got out of the car. Michael had lived there after college and has always told me "Once you go there, you will want to move there."

He was right.

We settled into the house we rented with my friend Sandy and had barbecues and pool parties all the time. Even Skilo seemed relaxed. Michael and I were finally on vacation. His company had an office out there, so he got to stay even longer than expected.

I finally got to meet the great group of friends Alex had made, and they were at the house every free moment they had.

When Mike arrived, there was none of the anger, fighting, or tiptoeing around each other that we had all grown accustomed to when we got together. The heaviness was gone, and we all felt it.

There was a sense of calm and togetherness for our family. As I watched Alex and Mike floating around in the pool one day, I laid there trying to remember the last time I felt so calm. We were still a long way from where we wanted to be, especially financially, but none of that mattered. I felt that we could get through anything. We had lost a few years to this crisis, and I was eager to catch up with all of those years on this family vacation. Family is everything. Sitting there watching my kids together made me realize even more what matters in my life.

I still scold myself for how stupid I was to ignore the signs. I am still angry with myself for not wanting anyone to know. Even on the happiest day, I know I will deal with this forever.

I have quite a few friends who have tried so hard to help their own kids and sent them off to all kinds of places against their will. It never seems to work. Mike tries to reassure me that no matter what I did, it wouldn't have mattered if he wasn't ready either. I hope he is right. And not just protecting me from the truth.

I've learned that the most important thing family members can do while we are waiting for the addict to want the help is to help ourselves. We cannot handle what is happening without getting help. If we do not understand what addiction is, we cannot help our children. The anger and hatred and war we wage is not against our children but against the real enemy—addiction itself. A family must join forces for the battle, helping each other, not just the addict.

It was very difficult as a parent to not become addicted to my child's addiction.

That is no way to live but at the same time very difficult to avoid. Awareness is crucial for success. I fell into this dark pit, but once I realized it, I started to pull myself out by focusing on anything else other than worrying about my son and the possibility of relapse.

I had wondered before Mike arrived how he would handle people drinking at the cookouts. I asked him before he came to LA if he wanted me to remove the alcohol from the house. He just laughed.

"Of course not," he said.

We talked about how impossible it was to remove all the drugs and alcohol from the world.

Positive thinking is more important than I ever thought it could be. I started to focus on the dog show for the first time in a long time. I fought through the guilt I'd felt for turning down the first offer. I needed to take the advice that I so freely handed out to everyone else. I would constantly say, "Nothing is going to fall in your lap if you just wait around for things to happen. Get up off your ass and go make something happen."

I started thinking about my own faith again and how I was going to find it. Was that black cloud still hovering?

But it seemed like all my positive thinking was helping. The following week I was sitting in Beverly Hills across from one of the biggest managers in Hollywood. She loves dogs and loved my show idea. The best part? She congratulated me for not losing sight of my concept and selling it as something I never wanted it to be. Staying true to my project was the smartest thing I could have done, and she wanted to represent my show because she believed in it.

This was the boost I needed. Having someone this important in the industry believe in me restored my faith. Brimming with confidence, and refreshed from a vacation with my whole family, I wanted to focus on spending quality time with my daughter. She had waited three years for some attention from her mother, and now I was in the right place to give it to her. After Michael flew back to New York, it was just the two of us. Seemed like things were turning the corner for us all.

For the next few weeks, Alex and I were glued at the hip. We went to flea markets, dinners, and shops and tore her apartment apart cleaning, reorganizing, and decorating. Alex had gotten me tickets to Ellen, Chelsea Lately, Jimmy Kimmel, The Fashion Police, and a bunch of other shows. At the Jimmy Kimmel show, Alex had me called on stage, and I was given a microphone to get the audience all riled up before the show started. She is a big troublemaker, just like her mom. I know that as a priest's daughter I have a bit of the devil in me (in a good way), and it was obvious to me that it had passed on to my daughter as well.

We had an amazing rest of the trip together. I was falling in love with California, and I didn't want to leave my daughter.

We decided to get one last mani-pedi at her favorite nail salon before I hit the road to drive back to New York with my friend Paul and Skilo. I almost cancelled the appointment but luckily I didn't. I never could have seen what was coming when I walked into that nail salon in West Hollywood.

The salon was very busy, so I had the good fortune of getting a pedicure by the owner of the salon. My daughter had been a customer there since she moved to Los Angeles. All the manicurists knew and liked her, so I received special treatment.

While sitting there with my feet soaking in the tub of soapy water, I noticed a woman across the room staring at me. I looked away, then looked back, and she continued staring at me. Even when I looked straight at her, she never flinched. She actually smiled and waved at me. I assumed she thought I was cute, so I ignored her and chatted with the owner of the salon. When I looked up again, she was standing right next to me.

She handed me a piece of paper with her name and phone number written on it and said, "I'm really sorry that I was staring at you, but there's something you need to know. Please call me when you are done here, and I'll be waiting at a café across the street. Let's grab a coffee and let me tell you something you definitely need to hear."

I looked at the salon owner as she watched the woman leave her place. I thought she was hitting on me and was giggling to myself about how different LA was.

"She has been coming here for almost ten years now, and I have never seen her do that before," the owner said, shaking her head.

"What? Hit on a stranger?" I was feeling pretty confident now that the woman was gone.

The owner laughed. "She isn't interested in dating you; she is a very famous psychic. I would definitely meet with her and see what she has to say." Her tone had turned serious.

Though slightly disappointed it hadn't been a romantic interest, I was intrigued. I called her as soon as I was finished, and we agreed to meet.

"Are you Greek?" she asked.

"Yes. Why?"

"Do you believe in the mati, the evil eye? Do you have a son and a daughter?"

"Yes." I couldn't take my eyes off her.

"Did your father come to this country at a very young age? Are you here visiting and working on three different projects, one of which is with someone with the initials M. M.? Did your parents marry at a very young age? Does one of your children suffer from addiction?"

Again, I said yes.

Then she said, "I couldn't stop looking at you in the salon because you have a huge sphere of stars spinning around you."

"I do?" I felt dizzy. How could this woman know so much about me?

She nodded. "We are about the same age, and I'm Greek as well. It's awesome that at this age you are embarking on an amazing journey. There is something wonderful about to happen to you, but there is something blocking the stars from bursting free. More importantly, I have reason to believe that you can help your children with their problems if you do what I tell you to do."

She had me hanging on every word. Especially when she mentioned helping my children. I was ready to do whatever she said especially when she mentioned "addiction."

I just prayed it didn't involve getting on an airplane. It's my greatest fear.

She then proceeded to tell me that there was a woman from Greece who was tremendously jealous of my mother because she was the reason my father never went back to Greece. "The time this woman came here to visit your parents in 1960, she put a hex (the Mati) on your mother without her knowledge. At that time your mother was pregnant with you."

She continued. "The spell has passed to you and to your own children, which may explain the addiction. There are only two ways to remove this evil. One way to do it is to see a powerful psychic that can remove the spell by channeling. The other way is to have a powerful priest read the removal prayer. Do you go to church? Do you know any priests to read the prayers?"

I had never told her that my father was a priest and that the reason he came to the United States so young was to attend the seminary in Boston. I told her I knew plenty of priests and bishops. She urged me to ask one of them as soon as I was back in New York. I thanked her, still dazed at all she said. She would not take any money from me. She said she just wanted to help another mother.

Once I got back to New York, I called the person I trusted most to see what his thoughts were about the "curse." He is my bishop, but I cannot name him. I've known him since I was a teenager, and he had been very close to my mother. He's always known I'm a bit of a wild child, and when I told him this story, he told me I was nuts.

His argument against the mati was, "If you believe in God, no one can wish ill upon you. God is stronger than the devil. Your mother was a woman of great faith. Who could this woman possibly be that would wish ill so strongly on her?"

I had spent so much time asking myself these questions, and I had all the answers. I shared my thoughts with him, and there was silence on the other end of the line. I knew he understood what my reasons were for questioning it all. Finally, he said, "Meet me at two on Wednesday."

That Wednesday in July, on a hot summer day, my faith changed significantly.

After my bishop stacked up the books he would be reading from, he started to fold the robes we would carry to his chapel. Beautiful gilded robes, each a different vibrant color. I was having flashbacks to when I was a little girl and would help my father fold the same types of robes. I was feeling very emotional and felt that I had done everything possible as a mother to help my son battle addiction. But the psychics' words kept tugging at me. I couldn't ignore the fact that maybe there was something more powerful that I didn't address. She had known too much and, as I'd learned, I knew absolutely nothing.

In my lifetime, I've seen the most stunning churches and cathedrals, but nothing was as beautiful as this hidden little chapel we were about to enter. The bishop opened the door and tears filled my eyes as warmth rapidly rose through my body. It was as if someone flipped a switch to make me instantly cry.

Stepping through the doorway, I felt warmth and love all around me. The only way I can describe what I felt was that it was as if I was entering a mother's womb. I felt completely isolated and safe. Everything was made of white marble, and there were beautiful hand-painted icons throughout the chapel. There was the most beautiful icon of the most important mother of all that I had ever seen. The Virgin Mary. I felt weakness and strength all at the same time and wished I could lock myself in this chapel and never have to come out.

It was so peaceful that I could actually hear the whisper of the burning candles. The floating scent of incense was wrapping itself around me like a mother's arms around her child. My senses had never been so heightened. The bishop told me to kneel in front of the Virgin Mary and to whisper the Lord's Prayer over and over again while he was preparing for the prayers.

A few minutes later, through my whispering, I suddenly stopped and stood very still. I was afraid to move for fear of anything changing. A scent had slowly drifted into the chapel. I held my breath, petrified that it would disappear as quickly as it had appeared. I recognized it immediately. It was the strongest memory I hold on to.

It was my mother.

It was her scent.

I know it well. It's on her robe that I keep zipped up tight, which I only open and close very quickly when I need to smell that scent. It's on her favorite pin that I have in her velvet-lined jewelry box. It's on her silk scarf that I still wear after all the years of her passing.

She was in the chapel with us now. I knew it. I felt it. It was real.

I turned and looked at the bishop. I didn't know if I should say anything since he already thought I was a little crazy. I smiled to myself when I realized he was experiencing the same thing. He stopped and looked around. He was sniffing the air and then he looked at me and asked, "Did you just put on perfume?"

I shook my head. "No," I whispered.

He looked confused. "I smell a very familiar scent. I can't place it and don't know where it's coming from," he said. He just kept looking at me.

"It's my mother," I said.

As soon as I said it, he knew. His eyes welled up and he said, "You are right. She is here." He had been so close to my mother when he was a young deacon that he remembered it as well.

197

I knelt and said the Lord's Prayer over and over again as he recited the prayers in Greek and in English. He was saying my children's names over and over again.

At the same time, he laid the beautiful heavy robes over me in layers. He placed what must have been six or seven layers of robes over me. I was crying, sweating, and feeling my mother all around me. My blood was pumping through my veins as he kept denouncing the devil and saying "Alexandra" and "Michael" over and over again. It felt like it went on forever. I didn't want it to end. Then, everything stopped. He lifted the vestments off of me one at a time. When he was finished, I stood up. I was soaked. The sweat and tears and my mother's scent were all mixed together, and I felt intoxicated.

I stood there staring at the candles burning as if in a trance. Neither of us said a word as I started to excessively yawn over and over again. The bishop asked, "Are you tired?"

"No, I don't know what's wrong with me." These were not typical yawns. They felt as if they were coming from the soles of my feet and sucked the air out of my entire body. I actually felt dizzy and wanted it to stop. It was scary because it felt like nothing I'd ever experienced before. It was so powerful that I was angry because it was breaking my focus on how I was feeling. It was breaking my wanting to reach out and feel my mother as I kept trying to breathe her in.

The bishop pulled a book out from the stack he had been reading the prayers from and flipped through it, looking for something. He read from a chapter about what can happen in different cultures when prayers are read to remove the evil eye from one's spirit. Then he said, "Now listen carefully." He read aloud that if in fact the prayers are successful, the ancient Greeks believe the way the spell leaves the physical body is through excessive yawning.

I was speechless. Then, just like that, the scent disappeared as quickly as it had appeared.

I didn't know how to feel. I was still so emotional knowing that my mother was in that chapel with us. He walked me out and up to the front door of the building. When he pushed it open, the scene outside was surreal. I felt as if I was having an out of body experience, until a wild gust of wind hit me in the face.

The sky was pitch black and the wind howled like crazy. Thunder and lightning had just started as we stood staring out the door. Before I stepped outside, I looked to the bishop. His black robe was blowing from the wind. It felt like a scene in a movie. I whispered into his ear, "Thank you for doing this for me and my family. It was the most amazing thing that has ever happened to me in my life. I am so glad you said yes."

He looked down at me. His eyes were glistening. "So am I, Anita. So am I. You did what you did for your children, and your mother was with you the entire time. There is no power greater than a mother's love." He looked out at the black sky. "I will remember this day forever."

I watched him close the door from the backseat of the cab. As we pulled away, I knew I would remember it forever as well.

I kept waiting for good things to happen to my family in the weeks following the bishop's prayers. Every time the bell rang, I thought I would see the Publisher's Clearing House van and a guy holding balloons with a check for a million dollars with our names on it. That never happened.

The expression "God doesn't give us anything we cannot handle" proved to be true for our family. But in August 2012, when I found a large lump in Skilo's mouth, I raised my hands up to heaven and said out loud, "Oh God, now what?"

We hoped it was just an infection, but after several tests and biopsies, we were told that she had a rapidly spreading cancer that would take her from us in the next few months. Skilo had been my crutch for the last few years; she was eighty-five pounds of pure love that I squeezed and hugged every chance I got. My loyal companion was only eight years old.

Michael and I were terrified and took her to an oncologist, where she verified the diagnosis. We were crushed. How could this be? Please God, not now!

We then met with a surgeon who said Skilo needed surgery immediately. They would remove a large part of her jaw followed by chemotherapy and radiation. She was going to be put through hell, with no guarantee of survival. Michael and I stood helplessly when they led Skilo away to prepare her for surgery. We felt that something was wrong. As we walked toward the elevator to leave, we looked at one another and said in unison, "Let's get Skilo and get out of here." It was a directive neither of us could ignore. We marched back in and told the attendants that we wanted our dog back. Skilo was not going to live her last few months with half a jaw, unable to run around Central Park chasing squirrels because of the chemo.

We drove home to our apartment, Skilo panting and wagging her tail in relief, in silence.

Many months later, I was in the park with a few girlfriends when we ran into the veterinary oncologist. Skilo was running around and playing with the energy of a puppy. The doctor observed Skilo's frolicking in complete disbelief. "Your dog is a medical miracle." As she examined Skilo's neck and throat, she searched through her mouth for the original tumors. She looked up at me and asked what we had done for her. I told her that Father Nathanael, my priest and dear friend, had blessed her every time he saw her. And then my friend Louise chimed in. "Skilo also had a private blessing from my bishop at the blessing of the animals."

The doctor cocked her head to the side and looked at both of us. "What exactly is that?" she asked.

Louise and my husband had taken Skilo to the blessing of the animals at St. John the Divine here in New York City. Llamas, pigs, camels, cats, bunnies, snakes, and sheep were all piled into the cathedral that day. When Michael and Louise went up to the bishop for communion, Louise asked the bishop for a private blessing for Skilo because she was so sick. He obliged and placed a hand on her head while reading a special prayer. As Louise explained this to my oncologist, I watched for any sign of disapproval. Instead she lowered her head as if she knew exactly what he was doing. My little girl was receptive to the power of prayer.

She got down on the ground with Skilo and searched through her mouth and felt all over her body. When finished, she looked up at us, her eyes filled with tears. "I can't find the growth or anything else for that matter. There is nothing here."

"Really?" I felt myself starting to cry.

"I'm putting my money on the prayers." She played with Skilo's floppy ears for a few more seconds before getting up and brushing herself off. On cue, Skilo darted off after a squirrel as if to demonstrate just how healthy she was.

The doctor was right. The why didn't matter. Michael and I had taken her home that day, and now here she was. And if we hadn't pulled her out of surgery that day, she wouldn't have been there trying to climb a tree. And she wouldn't have been there for Mike when he had to come and live with us a year later. Skilo wasn't ready to leave our family yet. We needed her, and she knew it.

Everything had changed in my life while going through my son's addiction and treatment. Everywhere I turned, everything was different. Except for the family dog, Skilo.

My loyal dog was always by my side, as if she knew what I was going through. She would take me for walks in the park so I could clear my mind and lay at my feet as I wrote this story. She would nuzzle up against my husband when she knew he was feeling lost and confused and put her head in my lap when I thought I couldn't take it anymore. She would do funny things as if on cue just to make us laugh when we thought we had no smiles left. She got me through it all because she was the one familiar thing in my life that never left my side. Her job was to make sure we got through each day before snuggling in next to us in bed at night. She would get up the next morning with her ears at attention, watching and waiting to see who needed her kisses, a warm snout to rub, or a long walk to take.

There were times I would just lie on the floor from exhaustion and sob when things were at their worst.

Skilo would plop her eighty-five pounds of love and warmth down right on top of me, covering me the same way I used to cover my children with their baby blankets. It was her way of protecting me, just like the blankets did all those years ago. She was behaving like any mother would. She was not the puppy in the pack anymore; her role had changed as well, and she was a mom. I believe it's true that all females have that mother gene and just want to take care of those they love. She was a female dog and her loyalty had no boundaries.

CHAPTER 13

BLOODSUCKER

Anita

Things had been so calm, as if our family had finally turned a corner and could get around to spending time together again without a cloud hanging over everything. Michael and I were in the garden behind our apartment one night with Joanie, enjoying a beautiful summer night, when the phone rang.

"Hey, Mom." It was Mike. "I'm at Baylor Hospital in Dallas."

The first thing I thought was, *He's relapsed.* "What the hell happened?" I demanded. The mood in the garden turned on a dime. It was like every day for the last three years had never happened.

"I had some kind of a seizure," he said. "I collapsed after practice and had to be carried out of the apartment and taken to the hospital."

205

"Are you doing drugs again?" I asked, terrified of what I assumed would be his answer.

"No, Mom. I swear." He sounded scared. Something I'd never heard when he'd been lying for all those years. While I wanted to believe him that it wasn't drug related, it was the first and only conclusion I allowed myself to come to.

Later that night, Mike's doctor called and told us it had been really hot all week in Dallas, so it was possible he had heat stroke. They were going to try to rehydrate him but were troubled by the seizure. The doctor mentioned postconcussion syndrome and said they were going to do a battery of tests, including a handful of blood tests. She said that Mike had such severe migraines that he needed to be put on pain medication. My heart stopped. Pain medication? Oh God, no.

I didn't know what to do. I assumed my son would never be able to touch even so much as a children's Tylenol again. I didn't want him to suffer, but I was frozen in fear with the idea of him relapsing. I called every doctor I knew, and I called his councilor at Caron. They all assured me that if the pain medication was being monitored, it was fine for him to take it.

"Your son is refusing the meds, Mrs. Devlin," the doctor said.

Mike

After moving back to Dallas from New York in February 2012, everything began to run smoothly, if not better. For that next year, everything was as great as it could have possibly been. We were traveling for lacrosse tournaments to Colorado, North Carolina, and more. Every day I was able to be of service to other young men like myself, especially working at the Gaston House. I had applied to school and really felt a great desire to finally go back and get my degree. As I said, everything was great. I was back with my community and friends and felt even more comfortable than I had in my first year of sobriety.

What happened next is something I could never have seen coming.

As the summer began in 2013, so did our extensive lacrosse program. We were beginning practices every day and preparing for the multiple travel tournaments we would have that summer. One day I began noticing some tremors in my hand that I could not consciously control.

Of course I never went to see any doctor, thinking that it was nothing and I could tough it out. Nevertheless, Friday morning came and these tremors began to become more severe, and not only that but I had a sensation of pins and needles up through my wrist.

During practice, I knew something was not right. Dizzy spells and tremors began to attack my body from all angles. The pins and needles in my hand began to turn into a painful numbness, as if the lack of feeling manifested as an alarm telling my brain that something was wrong. As the other coach and I were demonstrating a drill, he threw the ball over to me. When the ball hit my lacrosse stick, I could feel the vibrations travel through the shaft and into my hand. The pain was so shocking and severe that I dropped my stick on the ground. Coach and I looked at each other confused, and at that moment we decided it was a good idea to head home.

Fear started to creep in as to what the hell could have been going on. Was it dehydration of some sort, perhaps a heat stroke, or was this the end and I was about to die? All sorts of crazy thoughts crept into my mind before I felt my mind actually begin to slip away. I returned to the Gaston House, where the residents were in a Friday night house meeting. While sitting in my apartment, my feet began to tingle, followed by sharp pins and needles, which shot up my entire legs until it turned into complete numbness. To top it off, my vision split into two images, one of which was in only black and white. I knew something was seriously wrong at this point, and I somehow managed to shoot an SOS text out to two of my coworkers and friends who were running the house meeting.

What came next is all a blur to me, mainly because I was found unconscious on my bathroom floor. Jared and Caleb, my friends, came to my rescue to find me laid out on the floor with pee-covered pants. I can remember coming to a little bit, but I had no idea what was going on. Jared said something about calling an ambulance and immediately after said, "Fuck it," as he threw me over his shoulder and carried me to his car. Only a true friend would carry someone over their shoulder while they were completely soaked in their own urine.

They finally brought me to my own ER room with a bed and began checking my vitals and running tests. As the tests continued and hours went by, my mind began to clear up and my ability to speak came back to me. It was not perfect, but it was there. They ran every test they could. Blood tests, urine, CT scans, MRIs, and even the greatly feared spinal tap.

With having all these tests run, the hospital decided to admit me into their care. My good friend, David, knowing how petrified I was, decided to stay with me.

The next day everything seemed to be OK as far as tests went. They could not find anything too apparent, which was kind of relieving and concerning at the same time. Seizures, postconcussive syndrome, or even multiple sclerosis were possible diagnoses at this point, however nothing was definite. The doctor told me I could be released the next day since nothing was popping up.

That night when I went to bed, I began to feel a dizzy and nauseating sensation cloud me. I got up to throw up in the bathroom, where I began to lose my balance and tried to grab onto a safety railing. I can remember blacking out and seeing a big flash. I came to in a puddle of blood and my head in a nurse's lap as she held me and told me I was OK. They returned me to bed and had me sign a magical contract stating that I would not fall again while at the hospital.

This fall not only extended my stay at the hospital in Dallas but also added more tests for them to perform on me. One included an EEG, where they attached a series of wires to my head in order to monitor brain activity. Maybe it was the head injury, or perhaps just whatever was attacking my body, but at this point my mind was slipping away. At certain points I could not recall who I was, where I was, or even who the people were around me. Nobody knew what was going on. I think that was the worst part. The doctors could not come to a definite diagnosis as to what this was or how to treat it. After five days at the hospital and multiple scans, the neurologist concluded that it may be postconcussive syndrome and warned me that hitting my head again could cause some irreversible damage. I felt like a totally different person. I felt like I was losing my mind and quickly slipping into insanity.

When they finally discharged me from the hospital, I traveled to New York to spend time with my family. Upon arrival to New York, I met my mother and father at home, who were extremely worried when they saw how I looked. The plan was to stay rested and nourished while I continued to recover.

My dad explains it as the sound of a ton of bricks hitting the kitchen floor one night at my aunt's house.

I ended up in the ER with excruciating pain radiating from my head that had been there since my last hospital visit. I could not concentrate, nor even keep my right eye open. The doctors wanted to give me narcotics since they had tried some other options and nothing seemed to work. I can remember my mother freaking out and even calling my boss and my old councilors to ask if this was all right, considering I was a drug addict. He reassured her that these precautions needed to be taken sometimes, even if we have recovered from addiction or alcoholism. I cannot imagine what my mother must have been feeling telling the doctors to give me something for the pain.

A couple days later I finally got in to see one of the best neurologists in the city to hopefully find some clarification. I was scared. No one knew what was going on with me. Every test came back clear, and I seemed like a healthy human being. I was sick of being in hospital beds with wires attached to my head for days and being woken up every hour for tests. At least this is what I blamed my anger on, for in reality my fear and pain that I was not dealing with began to manifest as anger. I was becoming restless, irritable, and discontent once again and wanted nothing to do with anyone. I was taking all my anger out on my family, even on my sister who had flown in from California because she was worried about me.

The day after I was released from the hospital with no real diagnosis, I received a call from the Dallas

Department of Health about some hospital test results that had been taken weeks earlier. "Mr. Devlin, we have a record here that you tested positive for West Nile virus," the caller stated. West Nile? I thought that is where you get a fever, aches, chills, and all that good stuff. Well, after speaking with the neurologist, it finally all made sense. An extremely small percentage of people infected with West Nile will get a neurological infection such as encephalitis or meningitis. Symptoms include convulsions, numbness, partial paralysis, temporary blindness, tremors, extreme headaches, and more. It was every symptom I had been experiencing.

I couldn't believe that all of this was happening to me because of one little mosquito.

I was two weeks back into the swing of things in Texas, and I was feeling almost 100 percent once again. Out of nowhere I ended up having three more episodes from the West Nile in four days, consisting of blackouts and convulsions and temporary blindness. I ended up going back to New York this time to really rest and get back up to speed. My mother and I had a great conversation at one point and really were able to get on the same page as each other. We always had butted heads here and there my whole life, however for this five weeks, we did not once have any controversy. Even my fear of her being too overbearing and wanting to nurse me to health did not come true. In fact, she was helpful in making sure I was taking all the right precautions, but left it up to me to take care of them.

Containment has always been one of my biggest struggles. Often times I get ahead of myself, and rush to get into the next step of life. The problem with this is that I act too quickly, and before I know it, I find myself in a position where not everything is as I planned. The present can often slip away from me, and the future, which I am never even currently in, can become more important than where I am in this moment. That is exactly why I slipped into restlessness, irritability, and discontentedness while in the hospital. I was so consumed with my fear of the future and pain of the past that I could not focus and accept where I was at that moment. I was not willing to focus on my current health because I just wanted to be better. However, if I cannot continue to work on myself at the present moment, how could I expect to suddenly heal later?

The medical issues I got that summer were more of a gift than a burden in the long run. Struggling with my family became a good thing because we were able to grow and heal from it together, while our relationships in fact were strengthened.

I realized that anything can happen and interrupt my life at any time, so what is it worth to stress about the future when I am not even there yet? If I continue to focus on my mental, spiritual, and emotional health on a day-to-day basis, then the future should handle itself. My family and loved ones are the most important things to me in life. If I truly believe that, then I will continue to work through my own struggle and continue to maintain a healthy state of mind. Otherwise, how can I really care and be helpful to any of them if I do not first help myself? Not to say that any of us are perfect; however, it is the work that we put in, admitting our faults, and the willingness to change that makes the greatest difference.

Anita

I never thought my son's sobriety would be challenged by a mosquito bite. He was in excruciating pain because of the West Nile virus. His refusal to take pain medication was heroic and torturous all at the same time.

He came to stay with us for a few weeks of much-needed TLC. He didn't sleep because of the pain in his back and was highly agitated most of the time. This behavior brought back the awful memories of him as a drug user. I had to constantly remind myself that his current behavior had nothing to do with drugs. The virus was traveling through his nervous system, and there was no way of knowing where it would attack him next. I had to help him but not be the overbearing mother that I had been in the past. I had to be very cautious. He was scared and so was I. We all were petrified. I was afraid for him having this horrific illness but afraid of becoming the mother I once was, who treated my son like a little boy.

The doctor had made an appointment for Mike to meet with a pain management specialist once the West Nile diagnosis had come back from Dallas. I of course knew what that meant. We all knew what that meant. Pain pills. Those two words made me shudder. There had to be an alternative. I called nutritionists and body builders investigating how to strengthen his immune system and calm the inflammation in his spine. There had to be a way to get this disease under control holistically and without those damn pain meds.

Every day, I filled the fridge with the specially blended shakes I was told to make to pump up his immune system. I prepared mounds of spinach and protein every day and would leave everything out for him. It was his decision to eat and drink these concoctions without me pushing him to do it. I of course would check and be elated when I realized he was indeed drinking and eating it all. I knew Mike had no desire to see a pain management doctor. He wanted to get through this without having to take pills.

I reached out to an acupuncturist as a last resort and explained the situation. She wanted to get Mike in immediately for a special type of acupuncture called the "Bowen" treatment. We took him in that day for a treatment. This type of acupuncture is used for spinal inflammation and is done without using needles. Mike was skeptical but knew it was worth a try. She worked on him for two hours. When we got home, Mike fell asleep on the couch for hours and hours; it was the first solid sleep he'd had in weeks. When he finally woke up, he came into my room, and I immediately saw the change. He had color in his face and the permanent grimace was gone. "I don't know what she did to me, Mom, but it worked. It's a miracle."

He made another appointment with the acupuncturist but not before canceling the appointment with the pain management doctor. He kept pumping shakes and vitamins and greens into his system. He was feeling better each day. My son had returned. Again.

He dodged another bullet. He found a way out of resorting to pain pills. Mike chose to travel this road to recovery from West Nile, and for that I am so grateful. His treatment at Caron and Gaston House taught him that the strength to live without drugs lay within him.

I never would have thought that my son's sobriety would be challenged by a mosquito. The only things I know for certain are where we were yesterday, and where we are today. I have no control over what will happen tomorrow. I've learned to never let my faith in myself or my family be challenged ever again. I've learned how to be a better mother by not saying, "Do as I say, not as I do." I can't tell my children what to do, because in reality I don't know what's best for them, and I must acknowledge that. I can only try to be a good example for them to follow. Teaching them to struggle well, which may be the best lesson I can teach my children. Teaching myself to only be there when they need me and to not be there when they don't.

More important, I have learned that it's OK to take care of myself while being that same mother. I now know that I cannot give away all of my strength to others because I never know when I will need some for myself.

Thank you for letting us share.

AFTERWORD

I had told my son three years ago that I thought we should write a book together about our story of addiction and family. It seemed like a good idea at the time, but never having written anything other than a shopping list, I had no idea where to begin. I would sit staring at my laptop for weeks on end without ever typing a word.

One night while walking home in the dead of winter, I had a burning sensation exploding in my body. I peeled off my scarf and jacket and gloves feeling as if I had a terrible sunburn over my entire body. Once home, I took the coldest shower I could stand and even after finishing, I was still sweating. Something pushed me to sit at my desk and start writing my story. I was having these ridiculous hot flashes. They would surge through my body as I sat typing, making me feel like I was going to burst into flames. I felt as if I were on fire both creatively and physically at the same time. Just like that, my thoughts were flying through my fingers onto a page in front of me.

This was how I came up with the name for my blog, *Onfireatfifty,* which I had been told to create before writing the book to gain some recognition in the literary space. I asked some friends to start writing for it as well and to share their life experiences with the audience I was trying to build. All of the women who wrote for the blog were so inspirational that we ended up with tens of thousands of followers. The reason why was obvious. No one wants to feel alone when dealing with a life struggle. Women need to share experiences and support one another in times of trouble. This is how I came to write my first blog post about addiction, titled "No Room for Judgment." I was petrified to post the first public view into my private story of my child's addiction. The overwhelming response I received to that post fueled my desire to get this book written. As much as mothers were writing to thank me for sharing my struggle, it was I who was grateful for them convincing me to tell the whole story.

I wrote two chapters and sent them to my son. The next thing I knew, he sent back two chapters of his own. As I read his words, I began to feel sick. I thought that writing this together would be therapeutic, but I felt as if I had made a terrible mistake. I didn't want to know any of the details of his past besides the ones he had already told us. I didn't want to know or remember any of the things that had happened back then and started thinking that maybe writing a book together wasn't such a great idea. The worst part of it all was that as Mike and I started to work on the book together, I came to a blinding realization.

I was trying to forget what Mike couldn't remember.

I didn't like the way that made me feel.

I had to remind myself that it was all in the past. I had to think of that blog post and believe that maybe some of the things we went through would help someone else, so I kept writing. We had to tell the truth when sharing his story, or none of it would matter. I felt ashamed at times but realized that the only thing I should have felt shame for was ignoring all the signs years ago.

I should have been ashamed of myself for worrying about what other people would think instead of helping my only son.

Before and during the writing process, I made a point to stay away from reading books written by parents about addiction. I wanted to make sure my words were my own. Now that I've finished, I've started to read the stack that I have by my bedside and everyone's story is so similar. The names are different but many of the beginnings and middles are the same. None of us know how our stories will end.

This story is not about my son or me. It is about something much bigger than any of us. It's about holding on to hope while struggling. Life doesn't stop happening just because there is an addict in the family. No one takes you off of a magic list that says nothing else bad can happen at once. My family experienced an avalanche of life's misfortunes all at the same time. We could have retreated and been defeated but instead found strength in each other and fought the battles together.

I had to struggle through a heart attack, financial ruin while losing my family home and face my youngest child's addiction all at once. At the same time, the depression and menopause kicked in while I was trying to figure out what I wanted to do for the rest of my life. Trust me. You can and will get through it all. You are not alone.

I've learned more about myself as a woman and as a mother than ever before. I have learned more about true friendship and now see who has been holding tight to the base of my life ladder, making sure I don't fall down. It's so clear to me now, that it's easy to be surrounded by people when everything is wonderful. It's easy to be surrounded by people when you are the well and everyone stops by to take a drink or fill their cup. It's easy to be the one to lend a hand or an ear. It's never been difficult to be that person.

What isn't easy is watching people disappear when your well runs dry and the walls start to crumble. When things don't go quite the way they were supposed to. When you have nothing to offer to help make someone else feel better anymore. When the party is over and you become the one who needs the strength or the hand or the ear. It isn't easy when the only sound you hear...is crickets.

The past few years have changed me in ways I never imagined. My concept of strength was skewed. I never realized how much strength it takes to admit you need help. I never had to ask before. Had I given so much of myself away that my reservoir of strength had dried up? I wondered if my need was masked. Did the courage I so easily handed out to others cause them to believe I could never be weak?

Although I can never be prepared for what life may throw on my path, I have reclaimed the things I need most to survive: my strength and my faith. The past few years have challenged my faith. I thought I had lost it along the way. It took some time, but halfway through I realized that it was *me* who was lost.

I will never forget the people in my life that never let go of my ladder, no matter how difficult it was to hold on to. Special thanks to the friends who helped us with the book, reading, editing, commenting and listening to me read pages out loud for the past two years. Without you (you know who you are) we never could have done it.

In loving memory of my godparents Seva and Al who passed away as we were writing this book.

May their memories be eternal.

In loving memory of Skilo, our family dog, who lost her battle with cancer last month.

We miss our beautiful girl.

EPILOGUE—CARON TREATMENT CENTERS

Anita and Mike Devlin have written a compelling book that gets at the raw and painful heart of family addiction and the hope and possibility of individual and family recovery.

At Caron Treatment Centers, we say, "The patient is the family and the family is the patient," *SOBER* demonstrates the ultimate truth of this belief, as well as our experience in treating alcoholism and drug addiction for nearly sixty years.

Even in America, the tragic and ironic fact of the thousands of families afflicted with addiction is that sadly, only 10 percent of those families will get some kind of treatment; and ironically, addiction is one of the most successfully treated chronic diseases. People, including family members of the addict, can and do recover and prosper.

Over the years, most of the attention toward treating this disease has focused on the identified patient, the person who is using drugs and alcohol, the one who is acting out. This behavior might include stealing from friends and loved ones, getting a DUI, failing out of school, and emergency room visits. For some individuals, the behavior may be less overt and more subtle. Adolescent and young adult women, for example, can be more prone to self-destructive behaviors such as isolation, cutting, and eating disorders.

Caron was one of the first addiction treatment centers to develop adequate family programs. Over time, we have discovered how each member of the family comes to his or her own belief and involvement in the process of recovery. In fact, each person must do his or her own work and transition attention away from the addict and toward personal issues such as codependency, destructive coping mechanisms, anxiety, and depression.

One of the central symptoms of addiction is the preoccupation with the addictive action; the next drink, the next drug of choice. At Caron, we believe it is also critical to treat co-occurring disorders for an addict to fully recover. Co-occurring disorders can range from general anxiety and depression to eating disorders, gambling, and sexual addiction. Gamblers and sex addicts, for example, are preoccupied with the next game, gamble, sexual partner, or experience. Family members who are close to the addict become just as, or even more, preoccupied with their addict: where they are, are they high, are they driving, are they in the hospital, jail, or worse...

SOBER offers a seldom-seen, inside look at these relationship dynamics. We see it from a mother's view and from the addict's perspective; a rare glimpse demonstrates this daily, all-consuming relationship, engendering fear, anger, despair, and high anxiety. Parental anxiety makes rational decision-making almost impossible.

Anita's story is a deep dive into these relationship dynamics, especially as a parent, where making the healthiest choice may actually be counterintuitive to what we as humans are compelled to do in our moments of anger and desperation.

Anxiety makes breathing tighter and more difficult and impairs judgment. Stigma and shame makes reaching out to others very difficult. Anita tells of being in the right place at the right time when she needed guidance on how to help Mike at a critical, potentially life or death moment. A friend convinced her that instead of writing Mike off at that moment, she needed to detach with love. "Just text him," her friend said. And she did. That was the catalyst for change in a seemingly unsolvable problem and the turning point for the Devlin family.

Furthermore, recovery from addiction, like any other chronic disease, requires ongoing attention. As we say in the twelve-step rooms, one day at a time, or an hour at a time. Relapse is always a possibility in the developmental, lifelong process. Caron's theme of Recovery for Life honors the chronic nature of addiction and the need for continued growth and wellness.

For the addicted person, relapse can be triggered by medical problems that involve pain, where unknowing doctors prescribe mood-altering chemicals, by difficult and dramatic relationship challenges or through career and educational disappointments. For the family member, not hearing from a loved one, issues of trust, holidays, and celebrations can all trigger a relapse. However, with the right treatment and ongoing support, individuals and their families can plan for challenging moments and create a safety net as they inevitably face difficulties in life.

In a broader, more positive light, addiction treatment offers an opportunity for intergenerational healing and the prevention of trauma to future generations. Anita, Mike, and their family embody this kind of commitment to the future.

Recovery starts with finding those moments of truth and gratitude, returning to the present moment, and taking a breath, with each of us doing our own work. The twelve steps are excellent guidelines, as they help us to identify our foibles, our character defects, and connections with others.

As a parent or sibling, we must shift our attention away from the addict and back to ourselves and find the balance between love and personal growth. We must continue to cultivate the ability to say no, even in the midst of our own guilt and feeling that as a parent we did not do enough or that we did too much. Al-Anon tells us that the only person we can change is ourselves, even though we try so hard to change others. When we realize how difficult it is to change our own self, we see how impossible it is to change anyone else.

Here are some thoughts and resources to consider if you or a loved one is facing these issues:

1. Don't wait to seek professional help. Addiction is a chronic and pervasive disease and will not go away on its own. You can always call Caron at 800-678-2332 or visit the website at http://www.caron.org. Another national and regional resource is the National Council on Alcoholism and Drug Dependence (NCADD) at 800-622-2255 or http://www.ncadd.org, and they can connect you to a trusted treatment provider in your area. The twelve-step groups are free and in every community, and you can find them online at http://www.aa.org.

2. If you are involved in a faith community, ask the leaders what they believe about alcoholism and addiction. If their response indicates that they believe addiction is a moral weakness and are not responsive—consider other educational support and resources and offer that education to the clergy.

3. If you are involved in an educational community, insist that the organization has appropriate services for kids, students, educators, and parents. Nearly 90 percent of addiction begins in adolescence, and the sooner the problem is identified, the sooner it is treated. Untreated addiction touches every facet of society, often with tragic results.

4. Some professions even have specific associations designed to support the members of that field and their families. Lawyers Concerned for Lawyers, for example, offers guidance and support for lawyers afflicted with addiction and mental health issues. Their website is http://www.lclpa.org/about/.

5. Talk to your family healthcare providers; ask them how they identify and recommend help for those affected by addiction.

6. Insist that your political leaders are aware that addiction is a treatable illness and that laws must reflect that belief. Our courts and jails are full of untreated addicts.

7. Continue to read about and discuss addiction. You will be surprised that introducing alcohol and drug problems into a conversation

almost always opens doors to potential healing situations.

8. And don't forget to breathe! You and your family are not alone. Recovery is possible and offers many individuals and their families a second chance at life.

David Rotenberg
Executive Vice President of Treatment
Caron Treatment Centers
Recovery For Life

Made in the USA
Middletown, DE
12 May 2015